"*Blessing in Disguise* is an extraordinary book by a very compassionate and artful researcher. Dr. Rommer brings light and love to the difficult area of less-than-positive near-death experiences, and she finds spiritual meaning and value in the most painful cases, the darkest circumstances, and transforms them into powerful lessons not only for the experiencers, but the readers as well. I highly recommend Blessing in Disguise to everyone who is following a spiritual path. "

—Bill Guggenheim
Author of *Hello from Heaven!*

"At last, a book that sheds light on the transforming powers of both negative and positive NDEs! In my opinion, both types of experiences are gifts from God, and there can be no greater study for our spiritual growth and understanding. A must read, especially for those who have yet to glimpse life on the other side."

—Betty J. Eadie
Author of *The Awakening Heart, The Ripple Effect,*
and *Embraced by the Light*

"To say I am thrilled with Barbara Rommer's Blessing in Disguise is an understatement. She has investigated an area of Near-Death studies which has been consistently avoided, ignored or missed by other researchers in the field. Her grace and compassion shine through each page as she also each page as she also explores the deeper spiritual issues of both the experience and its aftereffects."

—P. M.H. Atwater, Lh.D.
Author of *Coming Back to Life, Future Memory,*
Children of the New Millennium,
and *The Complete Idiot's Guide to Near-Death Experiences*

"Health professionals, and people in general, need to become more accepting of the unexplainable experiences which are a part of our lives. This book may help open minds to what occurs during the Near-Death Experience and, thereby, save lives."

—Bernie Siegel, MD
Author of *Love, Medicine & Miracles and Prescriptions for Living*

About the Author

Barbara Rommer is a physician, specializing in internal medicine, and has practiced in Fort Lauderdale, Florida, for more than twenty-five years. She is an active member of the International Association for Near-Death Studies, frequently lectures on the topic, and has had a number of articles published in medical or scientific journals. She has appeared on CBS' *48 Hours*, and on the *Montel Williams Show*.

Dr. Rommer began researching the subject of near-death experiences to allay her patients' fears of death. She has interviewed more than 300 individuals about their experiences, drawing from those accounts for some of the information in this book. She lectures extensively to hospice organizations and other groups.

To Write to the Author

If you wish to contact the author or would like more information about this book, please write to the author in care of Llewellyn Worldwide and we will forward your request. Both the author and publisher appreciate hearing from you and learning of your enjoyment of this book and how it has helped you. Llewellyn Worldwide cannot guarantee that every letter written to the author can be answered, but all will be forwarded. Please write to:

Barbara R. Rommer, M.D.
℅ Llewellyn Worldwide
P.O. Box 64383, Dept. K585–1
St. Paul, MN 55164-0383, U.S.A.

Please enclose a self-addressed stamped envelope for reply,
or $1.00 to cover costs. If outside U.S.A., enclose
international postal reply coupon.

Dr. Barbara Rommer is available for lectures, book signings, and media interviews by arrangement through Lisa Braun, Llewellyn Publications, at (800) 843-6666, ext. 8450, or by email at lisab@llewellyn.com.

Another Side of the Near-Death Experience

BLESSING
IN
DISGUISE

BARBARA R. ROMMER, M.D.

2000
Llewellyn Publications
St. Paul, Minnesota 55164-0383, U.S.A.

FIRST EDITION
Second Printing, 2000

Book design and editing by Connie Hill
Cover photo by Chris Grajczyk
Cover design by Lisa Novak

Library of Congress Cataloging-in-Publication Data
Rommer, Barbara R., 1944–
    Blessing in disguise : another side of the near death experience /
Barbara R. Rommer — 1st ed.
        p.   cm.
    Includes bibliographical references.
    ISBN 1-56718-585-1
    1. Near-death experiences—Case studies.   2. Near-death experiences—Psychological aspects. I. Title.
BF1045.N4 R66 2000
133.9'01'3—dc21   99-089967

Llewellyn Publications
A Division of Llewellyn Worldwide, Ltd.
P. O. Box 64383, Dept. K585–1
St. Paul, MN55164-0383, U.S.A.
www.llewellyn.com

 Printed in the United States of America

I dedicate this book to:

J. Jay Rommer, M.D.
(my father, who is now in spirit)
for giving me soul;

William ("Willy") Salvatore Pepitone
(my son)
for filling my heart with love;
and

Salvatore ("Sonny") William Pepitone
(my loving husband who is now in spirit)
who has been and always will be
the wind beneath my wings.

My life has been something of value
because of these three men.

Contents

Acknowledgments

The spiritual journey that I have traveled to complete this book has been over many roads, across many hills, even mountains, and heaven knows down into many valleys. I must say, though, that it has been a real hoot, a learning experience all the way. I feel so very blessed by everyone who has crossed my path. I have learned something from everyone. The big, big things that I learned were from those whom I shall mention.

First, I wish to thank every single one of the people who granted me their time, their stories, their words of wisdom, and their love and kindness. They received no remuneration. I must repeat to all of you one of my favorite quotes (I wish I knew who said it!):"You never know where your shadow will fall." The accounts that you all have shared will most certainly influence others by giving them comfort and touching their souls. I include also all of the people who have shared their stories at our South Florida IANDS group.

I am most grateful to all of my patients. It is the rapport and the love that we have for each other that drove me to undertake this endeavor. May this book in small part give you solace and help to abolish any fear that you may have of death. May you all truly live every day of your lives without fear.

Thank you to Dr. Raymond Moody, friend and mentor, and to his wife, Cheryl, for their encouragement and support. My special thanks to Dr. Bruce Greyson. I also thank Nancy Evans Bush. They have also been very supportive of this "new kid on the block." Their early work on distressing Near-Death Experiences certainly piqued my interest. Thank you to Dr. John Cleveland, another researcher and writer on the subject of NDEs. He unselfishly started me out on my interviews with the set of questions that he had used in his research. He also gave me my first opportunity to appear on the radio. He shall always be a close friend and mentor.

I consider Delphi, in McCaysville, Georgia, my spiritual home on earth, and send love and light to Marshall Smith, Patricia Hayes, Charles Nunn, Kimberly Panisset, Steve Smith, and every single person at Delphi. I must also include Arthur Ford, in spirit.

There are many others, without whose encouragement this book would not have come into existence: Jack Cummings Jr., Maureen T. O'Connor, Shannon Kreiter (the mother of my Godchild, Erin), Linda A. Vardaman, Connie Sterling, Dr. Marta Covache, Barbara Langer, Dr. Rudolph Frei (who gave me the first opportunity to discuss NDEs with my peers), Dr. Jonathan Harris, Dr. Tom Lescher, Dr. Ed Coopersmith, Mark Dissette, Dr. Gary Meller, Barbara Zimmerman, Sister Georgetta (for helping me locate research articles), and everyone else at Holy Cross Hospital. I also thank Jack Cuthrell, Bart Ostroff, Venetian Toastmasters Club, Steve and Melanie Camp, Conrad Adelman, Dick and Tara Sutphin (whose tapes I use for daily meditation), and David Z. Mason, my computer whiz kid. I wish that I could mention by name absolutely everybody, but that is impossible.

Special acknowledgment to Dr. Joyce Strom, my friend, mentor, and cofacilitator of South Florida IANDS, and to everyone else associated with the International Association for Near-Death Studies, especially Diane Corcoran, Ph.D. (president) and Elizabeth Fenske, Ph.D. (editor of *IANDS Vital Signs* publication). It is my honor and pleasure to serve on the Board of Directors of that prestigious association. Thanks, also, to Casey Blaine, Mr. Chris Carson, Mr. Boyce Batey, Colleen Dougher-Telcik (the journalist who urged me to submit this manuscript to Llewellyn Publications), journalists Trish Riley Rector and Annete Herman, and Richelle Doliner (Community Relations Coordinator at Borders Fort Lauderdale). Love and light go to Rosemary Banks.

My deep appreciation goes to all those wonderfully spiritual people at Llewellyn Publications, including Nancy Mostad, Connie Hill, Lisa Novak, Lisa Braun, and everyone else there who had a part in this project. I am honored to be associated with them.

My love and respect and thanks to my dear father, J. Jay Rommer M.D., for his legacy of love, generosity, honor, wisdom, and above all, faith. My deepest love and thanks to my dear husband, Salvatore William Pepitone, the love of my life, who has been my backbone and my pacemaker. I remain touched by his gentle grace and quiet strength. Those two gentle men, although now in spirit, are certainly here with me. That is a given.

Last, but certainly not least, my loving thanks to my sweet son, Willy, for it is surely from him that I have learned the most. Because he is blind, I have learned to look with my heart. I shall continue to feel honored to be his eyes. Because he is partially deaf, I have learned to communicate by my demeanor and actions. Far more important than all these things is that my handsome little angel has taught me the gifts of kindness, acceptance, and sincerity, and has taught me never, never to judge.

I thank you all with my heart and soul.

Barbara R, Rommer, M.D.

Fort Lauderdale, Florida

October, 1997

Foreword

*I*n this book, Dr. Barbara Rommer has assembled a wealth of fascinating new case material relating to one of the most important popular mysteries of our time—the Near-Death Experience. She has produced a penetrating and insightful study of distressing Near-Death Experiences and their aftereffects. Her book is a major contribution, because she has courageously ventured into uncharted territory and produced a preliminary road map giving clues to the solution of an exciting puzzle: What characteristics distinguish those who report alarming or negative Near-Death Experiences?

Dr. Rommer is a practicing internist and her medical wisdom shines through the pages of the book.

As the story unfolds, we see plainly that she is guided by her curiosity and her compassion for her patients, not the heavy-handed religiosity and ideological slant that, unfortunately, warped previous books on the subject of distressing NDEs. Dr. Rommer's purpose here is not to frighten readers into conformity with the author's religious doctrine, but rather to explore the meaning of other unfavorable visions in the lives of those who experience them.

It is interesting that Dr. Rommer finds that even the most horrifying Near-Death Experiences eventually have a positive spiritual outcome—they are "blessings in disguise." As such, her book is a fine addition to the inspirational literature on the subject of the meaning of human suffering. Dr. Rommer knows the meaning of the suffering she writes about, having recently undergone the loss of her beloved husband, and having the continuing responsibility of caring for a wonderful son who is handicapped and unable to care for himself.

This book is well worth the reading. It will very soon find a place on the required reading list for everyone with a serious, in-depth interest in extraordinary phenomena of human consciousness that attend the dying process. It brings a hopeful note into the bleakest situations. We find that human beings can bring back new meaning and new love, even from their descents into the darkest nights of the soul.

—Raymond A. Moody, M.D., Ph.D.
Anniston, Alabama

Introduction

*H*ave you ever grieved the loss of a loved one? Have you ever been close to death or thought about what happens when one dies? Do you fear death or fear the unknown? Do you do volunteer work with patients who are terminally ill? Have you ever lost a child or other loved one to a violent or otherwise traumatic death? Have you ever had a peaceful Near-Death Experience or a Less-Than-Positive Near-Death Experience? Do you have a child who has had a peaceful Near-Death Experience or a Less-Than-Positive Near-Death Experience? If you answered "yes" to any of these questions, then you will benefit from the information in this book.

Most people fear their own death and the death of their loved ones, in large part, because fear of death is fear of the unknown. For nearly thirty years I have cared for ill patients, many of them dying. It struck me early on, and saddened my heart, to realize that because of fear about the dying process and of what happens after dying, most people do not live life to the fullest. Fear of death causes fear of life. Thus, when I began this endeavor, it was with one simple goal in mind: to allay people's fears by reporting the experiences of those who had died and been resuscitated.

That is how it began. That is not how it ended. By the time I was ready to put my findings on paper, I had completed more than 300 in-depth interviews. While I cannot state absolutely that there is an afterlife, I can present overwhelming anecdotal evidence testifying to that probability. Perhaps we don't require absolute proof of an after-life. Perhaps that is where faith comes in. For many of us, a glimpse into what comes after offers the solace we seek in this life. Even if we cannot prove life after death, at least physicians know that anoxia, which causes unconsciousness preceding death, often also causes euphoria.

Personally, I began my spiritual quest as a child. I was blessed to have been the daughter of J. Jay Rommer, M.D., who was my men-tor, my friend, and my spiritual teacher. He was a very old soul. When I was only five years old he had his first major heart attack. I was protected from knowing anything about his illness, but I do remember being terribly afraid that he would die. At that time, for months and months, night after night, I would sneak into my bath-room late at night and cry. I stifled my tears in a towel so I wouldn't be heard. I thought it was my secret, until one night I shall never for-get. I was startled as the bathroom door opened and the light went on. There was my father, with tears in his eyes. He said: "Baby, we have to have a talk." I sat on the edge of the bed and Papa sat on the rocker. He said: "It hurts me to see you cry, my child. I know why you're crying. I know you're afraid something will happen to me, but I'm not going to die for a very long time. As long as you need me I will be here for you. But let me tell you about death so you won't ever fear it, and of this I am very, very certain. When someone dies, it's just like waking up from a dream, nothing more." It was many years before the light bulb went on in my head, making me realize that my father had obviously had a Near-Death Experience when he had that severe heart attack. He was speaking from personal knowl-edge of death.

Perhaps I became a physician in an effort to emulate my father. H
was very loved by his patients and set a wonderful example for me.
When Gallup polled scientists (including physicians), he found that
only 16 percent believe in life after death, as contrasted with 67 percent of the entire American population. I can explain why the attitude
of nonbelief occurred for most of us who attended medical school in
the 1960s. Medical training at that time provides a good study in sub-
jugation or denying one's spirituality. We were all in a constant state of
panic as a result of exhaustion, sleep deprivation, and absolute com-
petitiveness. At our very first class in the huge amphitheater the ten-
sion could be cut with a knife. Hardness of spirit was a defense mechanism fostered from the very moment the dean of students addressed
us, stating that he would see less than 70 percent of the class returning
for the second semester. The pressure was overwhelming. It seemed
from the start that compassion, empathy, love, and spirituality might
well be incompatible with a modern medical career.

All of our professors were in a publish-or-perish mode, living in a
state of high anxiety. Few displayed any warmth. I called my father,
crying, when a professor, who had no use for women in medicine,
admitted that he hoped that I would fail. (I was the only female in
my class.) He said: "You belong in the kitchen cooking for a husband
and family. Women don't belong in medicine. You lack the toughness it takes." Notice the word "toughness." I thought kindness and
empathy were more appropriate for a physician who would be caring
for ill, frightened patients.

Death was homogenized and purified to allow us to deal with it
simplistically in a nonpersonal and "safe," purely physiologic and
biologic way. Death was something to be avoided at all costs. The
death of a patient was regarded as our failure, regardless of the circumstances. Initially, death was confirmed by the absence of a heart
beat and breathing. Later on, legal issues complicated that, and a flat
EEG (brain wave tracing) was often added. In addition, criteria of a

specific number of minutes without breathing or a heart beat was considered. All these things encouraged most of us early on to cast aside our spirituality. Science became our security blanket. We learned to hide behind the rhetorical "show me" or "prove it to me" statements. We subconsciously constructed a wall between our right brain and our left brain.

In 1971, during my medical residency at the Manhattan Veteran's Administration Hospital, I heard my first account of a detailed Near-Death Experience. The patient had a massive heart attack which led to a cardiac arrest. In other words, his heart stopped beating, he stopped breathing, and was clinically dead. In those days it was very unusual to survive a cardiac arrest, and this patient would not have survived had it not been for a cardiology resident and vascular surgical resident being there at that moment, ready to "practice" open heart massage.

The most striking thing that I shall always remember was how very angry the patient felt about having been "brought back." I spoke with him at great length. I memorized his spiritual death experience, and then filed it away under "unexplained curiosities" in the memory bank located in the deep recesses of my brain. As time went on, that memory kept surfacing.

In my private medical practice, I have always felt great warmth and love for my patients. I have been very blessed to have wonderful patients with whom I've had an excellent rapport. My only sadness was the realization that most of them had an overwhelming fear of death. Many admitted that, because of their cultural and religious upbringing, they were programmed to "expect and fear retribution." Many, many times when I had a patient in a terminal state I would relate that gentleman's Near-Death Experience and then would tell them what my father had said about death. They received much comfort from that sharing. As each person listened with their heart I could see the fear leave their eyes.

As time went on I became driven to search out and speak with more people who had similar experiences. My quest for spiritual truth has taken me through thousands of hours poring over books, journals, and articles, and listening to tapes about Near-Death Experiences. My focus and clarity were sharpened by courses I attended at Delphi University in McCaysville, Georgia. Delphi is a private institution with programs in transpersonal studies (intuitive and spiritual sciences including mediumship) and alternative medical therapies, including spiritual healing techniques. There I experienced very accelerated spiritual growth.

I have been blessed to have had many phenomenal mentors. I also feel fortunate that researchers I have contacted regarding this subject have been wonderful and totally supportive. There is a saying that "when the student is ready the teacher will appear." Well, I was ready and over 300 teachers, i.e. all of my interviewees, appeared. Not only have I received knowledge and gained wisdom, but I have experienced significant healing, as well, and you may also.

There have been many stumbling blocks along the way, such as my father's death, my husband's illness and subsequent passage into spirit, and my son's multiple challenges. My little boy, Willy, is blind, has cerebral palsy, has a hearing impairment, is mentally retarded because of the sensory deficits, and cannot speak. All these things not only amplified my quest for truth, but ultimately gave me strength and confirmed my faith and knowledge that as spiritual beings we are all connected to each other and to our Creator.

I believe that the only part of us that dies is our physical body, once referred to as our "husk" by a Catholic priest who related his own Near-Death Experience to me. The body is physical matter, but is not our true essence. Our true essence, our soul, our spirit, our life force, and our very being, that part of us which has a personality, most probably does not die. I must admit that I have received what I consider to be confirmation of this from my husband, Salvatore (Sonny) Pepitone, who entered his spirit form on June 25, 1997.

By the time I had completed only twenty interviews, I realized that along with the pleasant Near-Death Experiences came accounts that were very frightening. As I accumulated more and more of the frightening ones, certain patterns evolved. Profoundly positive life-altering changes occurred as a result of these frightening experiences, and those changes were sometimes even more significant and longer-lasting than those that occurred after pleasant Near-Death Experiences. This very positive impact made the word "negative" (which has been applied to these events by other researchers) a misnomer. Therefore, I call them "Less-Than-Positive Near-Death Experiences," or LTPs, and they truly are a "Blessing in Disguise."

Initially, I had intended for my research to culminate in a book about the prototypical Near-Death Experience, using personal stories and illustrations. My plan changed when I realized the importance of focusing on these Less-Than-Positive Experiences, especially since there has been so little written about them. Data suggests that LTP experiences are far more common than current research suggests. The LTP experiencer needs to know that he or she is not alone. I also feel that everyone who vicariously experiences an LTP will grow spiritually, which makes each experience, therefore, a blessing to us all.

It is significant to note that a person does not need to undergo a Near-Death Experience or an LTP to learn the lessons and/or begin to heal. Studying these accounts has helped me begin to comprehend the essence of our true human nature. We are spiritual beings first, and physical beings second. With each LTP we are reminded of the reasons why we are here. We are here to learn, to teach, to make a positive difference, and to be of service to others. We are here to learn and practice unconditional love and forgiveness, and to reconnect with our Creator. We are not here to hurt ourselves or others. Life is a precious gift. We do not have a right to destroy it.

These events teach us that every second of our lifetime involves a choice. We are in control. We are in dominion. We can choose to live a life of fear, void of meaning, being a victim, and not fulfilling our purpose, or we can learn from our experiences and those of others and choose to walk in light, fulfilling our purposes. Our journeys matter. This lifetime is not about earning points for a bigger reward, because we will all eventually get the same reward. We were all born with this universal knowledge, but somehow we have forgotten it along the way. May this book act as a reminder and may it jog our memories.

I believe that when we entered this lifetime, we were provided with a general map. The course we take or route we choose is determined by us. The NDE (Near-Death Experience) and especially the LTP often shock a person into rerouting his or her journey. When a person changes his or her life and begins to take responsibility for every second and every action, one cannot help but positively influence others. This is the ripple effect.

By studying the Less-Than-Positive Experiences we, too, can bring about necessary changes in our own thinking, in our own way of viewing the world, and in our own lives. The Less-Than-Positive Experience is a spiritual wake-up call, causing the person to stop, look back, and review past choices. It can help him or her understand the consequences of those choices, reevaluate thought patterns and "glitches" in thinking or reasoning, and then make necessary changes where indicated. The LTP becomes the nexus point of that individual's path, causing him or her to change their walk and direction. I view it as the ultimate learning experience.

I firmly believe that both the pleasant Near-Death Experiences and the Less-Than-Positive Experiences most often occur because of the need or desire of the experiencer. With the LTP in particular, the need may be to bring one's attention to a past action, reaction, error in reasoning or judgment, or to a less-than-positive choice. Since we are all human, we have all made one or more less-than-positive decisions. That's how we learn, which is one of the reasons that we are here. I also believe that negative programming during childhood, as well as a Less-Than-Positive or fearful mindset just immediately prior to the experience can cause it to be of the Less-Than-Positive type.

Therefore, not only do I believe that it is the person who causes the LTP to happen, but he or she is also responsible for the type of imagery that occurs in the experience and the total content of it. In the LTP, we see what we need to see, hear what we need to hear, and feel what we need to feel in order to do those reevaluations. The cosmic forces, or universal consciousness, know what one unique thing a soul needs to expand its consciousness in order to be open to higher truths.

There are no trivial NDEs or LTPs. A brief episode can cause as great a transformation as a longer, more complex one. What one *needs* is what manifests. There can be confirmation of a belief, or there can be frank dissolution of a false belief. It is a true blessing when one's doubts, fears, and false beliefs are ultimately released.

It is tempting to think that a "mean" person will necessarily have a frightening or hellish experience, and a gentle, kind person have a blissful experience. Please believe me, that is absolutely not the case. Everyone has the potential of having an LTP. No one can live up to all of society's, our family's, and our own expectations completely. There is always something we might have done differently. We are all disappointed about choices we made in the past. I believe that if we do our life review, self-evaluation, and judging now, then we may avoid the need for an LTP experience. The LTP can be used as a starting point for therapy. A heart hardened by trauma and hurt can be transformed, allowing one to expand consciousness. In other words, all NDEs (including the frightening ones) bring about expanded awareness, which can have only positive results from a cosmic perspective. LTPs and NDEs can set individuals on a new path and reveal to them their own treasures and abilities. They can ultimately give comfort with reference to self- and universal forgiveness and nonjudgment, and can reaffirm the importance of the golden rule.

It is my hope and intention that people who have kept silent about having these types of experiences will read this and understand that they are not alone. May they receive insight, clarity, understanding, and comfort from this information. Rather than a tool of self-condemnation, the LTP experience is an instrument of growth, with the potential to bring about soul growth more rapidly than the transcendental light experiences.

People are essentially lying naked, bleeding, and bare when they expose themselves through their stories to a critical and often cynical world. I pray that you will all keep an open mind and listen with your heart and with awe to these accounts. It is out of the kindness of their hearts and with God's love that they share their very personal experiences.

Every single subject was personally interviewed by me, orally, either in person or on the telephone. The interviews ranged between forty-five minutes and eight hours in length. I also personally transcribed every single interview and reviewed all the medical records. Not one of these people were ever interviewed by any other researcher, since that was one of the criteria for entrance into my study. Many of the interviewees are my private medical patients, and I was present at the resuscitation of several of the experiencers.

It has been my honor and joy to do this study and contribute to the existing body of literature on the subject. I began this project with a love for my patients and the hope that I might help to allay their fear of death. I have gained more knowledge and wisdom and love for humankind than I had ever hoped for. If my readers take the lessons they read to heart they can change their own lives for the better. May this book not only ease your fear of death, but also give you peace and a better understanding of life.

ONE

Peaceful Near-Death Experiences Revisited

Kathi S. was twenty years old when she had her Near-Death Experience in 1963. She had put on a tremendous amount of weight after a divorce, so she "starved" herself for three months. After developing all of the possible complications, she was admitted to a hospital. It was not known that she was allergic to penicillin.

> They kept giving me more and more penicillin, then I became comatose. Suddenly I was up on the ceiling looking down at the nurse taking the vital signs, and she couldn't find my blood pressure. She buzzed somebody. I didn't go through any tunnels. I just turned over and I was in this beautiful place. I was in a garden, facing a three-tiered fountain. The water in the fountain just kind of sang. On the circle around this fountain were flowers of the most beautiful colors I've ever seen. There are no flowers like that on

You must never fear death, my child. Of this I am very, very sure. When one dies, it is just like waking up from a dream. Nothing more.

—J. Jay Rommer, M.D.

1

this planet. They vibrated. Everything vibrated of color. There was grass around it and three sidewalks coming up to it. The green grass was gorgeous, with beautiful hedges all around and big tall buildings to my right.

I felt total peace, total happiness, total harmony, and the highest ecstasy you could possibly imagine. It's an ecstasy that's higher than any type of high. I don't do drugs and have never done them. It's like when you play racquetball and get that euphoria, or dance for forever, or even have an awesome sexual experience with someone you're very much in love with. It's higher than that. It's the highest high of love you could possibly imagine. It's like you're totally enfolded in the arms of God, and you're home and you know you're home.

Periodically during this I would think about my body. You move as fast as thought, and I'd be back on the ceiling looking down. I heard the nurse say: "No, it doesn't look good." I saw the doctor inject this big syringe into my heart. I think it was adrenaline. Then I saw them shocking me. I saw my body jump up and down. Then I'd turn over and I'd be back in this beautiful garden again. One time I saw my mother crying at the end of the bed.

Back in the garden, I thought in my mind that this awesome place is home, and I'm going to just stay here forever. Then I heard this big booming voice, but there was no physical form. I didn't know if it was the voice of God or one of his right-hand angels. It resonated through me. The voice said: "You can stay here for a time, however if you stay here for too long then you're going to have to be born again." I said: "You mean like a baby in diapers?" The voice said: "Yes." Then I said: "Oh, no! I don't want to do that!" I spent all those years growing up and I'd have to go to school again and I'd have to do parental discipline and go through all the hassles that you have to go through growing up.

The next moment I was back in the body and I opened my eyes. The doctor was slapping me on the face. He said: "I thought I lost you!" I never discussed any of those things with anyone for many, many years. You asked me if I fear death. No, I don't. It is easier to die than to be born, but the fear is built into us. People need to know that when they die they'll just be home with God.

What is a Near-Death Experience?

According to IANDS, The International Association for Near-Death Studies, the definition of a Near-Death Experience, or NDE, is "an event or series of events that occurs in the absence of a heart beat and respiration." Nearly identical experiences can also occur with deep meditation, with severe physical stress such as trauma, accidents, surgery, and childbirth, and with physical exhaustion. It can also occur during emotional distress such as grieving, and with sleep deprivation, marathon running, and when one is just slipping into a deep sleep state. Kenneth Ring, a much-published researcher on NDEs, stated in his book *Heading Toward Omega* (Morrow, 1984): "What happens to an individual during an NDE is not unique to the moment of apparent imminent death. It is just that coming close to death is one of the very reliable triggers that sets off this kind of experience."

The term "Near-Death Experience" was coined by Dr. Raymond Moody in his book *Life After Life* (Bantam, 1975). Interest in the subject has escalated astronomically since that time. A 1982 Gallup poll estimated that over eight million Americans had Near-Death Experiences, or approximately 35 percent of those who had been in an imminent death situation. A 1992 updated poll estimated that there are thirteen million American experiencers. Preliminary findings of current studies suggest that between 9–15 percent of those people close to death have an NDE.

Near-Death Experiences have been described through history. In the Bible Paul describes his NDE. They have been written about in *The Tibetan Book of the Dead*, in Kabballistic teachings, in Mormon writings, and in Plato's *Republic*, to name a few. Pope Gregory the

Great, in the sixth century, reportedly sent out scribes to interview those who reported such events. Well-known people in history such as Carl Jung, Ernest Hemingway, Elisabeth Kübler-Ross, Thomas Edison, Benjamin Franklin, Elizabeth Barrett Browning, and Louisa May Alcott have all described their NDEs. I shall not go into the historical aspects of Near-Death Experiences because they have been so very well covered in many other books on the subject. I refer the reader to *Life After Life* by Dr. Raymond Moody and to *Closer to the Light* by Dr. Melvin Morse and Paul Perry (Random House, 1990).

NDEs and LTPs (Less-Than-Positive Near-Death Experiences) happen to people of all ages and all religions, even to people who profess to be agnostic or atheistic. They occur to people of all cultures, all economic backgrounds, and in all parts of the world. As we will soon see, the NDEs and LTPs are all described as a variation on a theme. The descriptions obviously reflect the cultural and religious circumstances of that person. For example, I interviewed several Native American experiencers who used terms very specific to their culture.

Underreported NDEs

Most people who have had these experiences do not readily speak about them because they fear being ostracized or being referred for psychiatric care. Fortunately, groups such as the International Association for Near-Death Studies support groups (such as South Florida IANDS, which I cofounded and cofacilitate) provide excellent forums for discussion with other experiencers. Many people who were not aware of NDEs report confusion after the event. Many people have told me that after their cardiac arrest and resuscitation, they were in such awe of what they had experienced that they tried to tell the physician and nurses, but were met instantaneously with cynicism. They kept silent from then on. One subject said he was told by a medical person that he "obviously had a loose thread in his fabric"!

I interviewed a Roman Catholic priest who had an NDE following a severe heart attack. He said to me:

> I wasn't sure, because you're a clinician and scientist, how you would be. I remember one time some physician heard me talking about it and he started to tell me about endorphins. I said: "Listen, I don't want to be flip with you, but if I tell you that I went through that door to that corridor, don't tell me that my endorphins exploded or there was a re-uptake or something, because I went through that door. This happened. It was not a dream. It was not an illusion or a fantasy. This happened."

A comedian, who looks and sounds like Jerry Lewis, had a cardiac and respiratory arrest following a heart attack in a Florida restaurant. He was successfully resuscitated, then taken to a hospital. He said:

> I told one person in the coronary care unit that I'd seen my mother and sister (both deceased) and she started to laugh. She asked me: "Did you see Clark Gable too?" After that I didn't tell anybody except my brother. I said to him: "I saw Mom and Sis." He said: "And did Mom ask you for money?" and laughed. So I haven't told anyone else except you.

Objective Evidence

Many people visit very distant locations during their NDE, with subsequent confirmation about what they described. The following account is particularly fascinating. It happened to Tony, the husband of Pat Meo, one of the nursing supervisors at Holy Cross Hospital in Fort Lauderdale.

Tony and Pat traveled from South Florida to Milwaukee for Tony's open-heart surgery. The afternoon following the surgery, his chest had to be reexplored in the operating room because of continued bleeding. While he was being reprepped, he had a cardiac and respiratory arrest. He was clinically dead for thirty minutes. His cardiac surgeon did an open heart massage, which was finally successful.

During this time Tony found himself first "standing" next to the surgeons who were trying to resuscitate him, and then he ascended to the top of the surgical suite. He understood what was happening and wondered if Pat knew what was going on. He immediately found himself in the surgical waiting room, watching her call up north on the telephone, crying. Whatever he thought immediately manifested. He thought that he "just wanted to go home to Florida," and suddenly he was there!

While home in Florida he "saw" all of the mail which had been taken in by the housesitter, strewn all over the dining room table. He accurately described all of the letters, bills, junk mail, and magazines. He was able to describe the housesitter's girlfriend in detail. Tony and Pat had not known of this young lady's existence. All of this was, of course, confirmed. Next, he went to New Jersey and "saw" some family members and old neighbors.

The transcendental part of his Near-Death Experience was also profound. Tony described the classic pearly gates, and also described reviewing what he considered to be several previous lifetimes. He then found himself, joined by a guardian angel, walking along a dirt path. When they came to a black wrought-iron gate, Tony rang the bell that was attached to a long rope. A "man who had a face that was a bright light" answered the ring of the bell, then told Tony he was expecting him and that he might enter, after verifying his name in a large book that he was carrying.

Tony said: "I was in the most beautiful place I had ever seen. It had a pure, pleasant, fresh, clean smell. I was pain free and totally happy. There were beautiful flowers of vibrant, vivid soft colors. A stream of crystal clear water was flowing down the mountain, the top of which protruded into the clouds." Tony felt that it was Saint Peter and four other robed people who escorted him up that mountain. When he stumbled several times, Saint Peter asked him: "Do you have a problem? You keep hesitating. Would you like to go back?"

Tony answered: "Yes," because his wife, Pat, and his family needed him. Saint Peter told him that he might go back, but that he would be returning on a specific date. He was also told of a mission that he was to accomplish.

He would never tell Pat either the projected date of his return or about his mission. Two-and-a-half years later, on August 29, Tony went into spirit. Two years after that, Pat was finally cleaning out his drawers. She found a small piece of paper, tucked in the back, with Tony's handwriting. It said: "Return date: August 29."

Dr. Kenneth Ring has been studying the Near-Death Experiences of people who have been blind since birth. Although congenitally blind, these people often describe things in tremendous detail as though they were sighted. Food for thought for the skeptics, I am sure. (This is particularly interesting to me because my son, Willy, is blind.)

Some experiencers are able to accurately describe their resuscitation in astounding detail, including the settings on the machines used to resuscitate them. They are often at eye level while observing the event. Dr. Michael Sabom contrasted how these experiencers, describing their own resuscitation, compared with a control group of intelligent people who were asked to invent a story about what they might expect to see in the same situation. The control group was unable to make up an accurate resuscitation story.

Some NDErs come back from the other realm with information that they could not have otherwise known. Gloria was a flight attendant, on layover in another country, when she had a respiratory arrest secondary to a severe allergic reaction. In the NDE, she found herself bathed in the loving light and was greeted by an older brother and her father, both deceased. She was also greeted by a young boy and was told that he was also her brother, and that he had died a few years prior to her birth. This was confirmed by her mother. No one had ever told Gloria of the existence of that brother, and there were no photos of him in the family albums.

I have interviewed many Near-Death Experiencers who reentered this lifetime cured of the physical illness that caused their death. I have painstakingly reviewed their complete hospital medical records. My cases include people who have come back totally healed of kidney failure, end-stage liver failure, aplastic anemia (bone marrow shutdown), legal blindness, pneumonia, and cancer.

I have also interviewed several people who, after being pronounced dead by trained medical personnel, were in that state for a very long time. Three people awoke in the hospital morgue. Another person reentered his life in a funeral parlor.

The "Usual" Elements of an NDE

Dr. Raymond Moody, in his book *Life After Life*, noted the striking similarity of NDE accounts and suggested that one can easily pick out fifteen elements that reoccur. This has continued to hold true in my own study. Those elements include: ineffability, hearing the news (of the subject's own death told by the physician, for example, to others in attendance), the pleasant feelings of peace and quiet, the noise (unusual auditory sensations), the dark tunnel, the out-of-the-body experience, and meeting others. The other elements include an encounter with a being of light, the life review, and the border or limit beyond which the subject may not go and still return to his body. There are many other elements which occur less frequently. I shall present these elements and their variations when I discuss the "typical" NDE.

An Example of Ineffability

"Ineffable" refers to the indescribable quality of the NDE. Most subjects state that our extremely limited vocabulary lacks the subtleties to adequately convey the event in words. This is so with both the usual NDEs and LTPs.

Sadhana was thirty-eight years old at the time of her profound NDE. She is a Native American, who has studied in India, and she currently lives in Taiwan. Her Near-Death Experience followed a cardiac arrest which resulted from severe dehydration and electrolyte imbalance due to dysentery. She found it very difficult, despite speaking several languages fluently, to explain adequately what she felt and observed. She stated:

> It was so incredibly profound. It was six months before I could speak to anybody about this. The vastness, the profoundness, the immensity, the exquisiteness was simply beyond human words. It still is, but at least I can use what I have to give you some clue. I can use the analogy that it's, like my words, like a reservoir trying to to come through this little kitchen tap. It's slow and it's painful. If you only see the kitchen tap, then you can't even imagine what a reservoir looks like. In fact, even your imagining of a reservoir would give you no clue of its . . . there we go again for words, I can't even say "immensity" because that's such a tiny, tiny word.

A "Typical" NDE

I feel that it is critically important for the reader to understand the "typical" NDE in order to fully grasp the impact of the LTP (Less-Than-Positive) experience. The "typical" Near-Death Experience refers to the oft-publicized, pleasant "illuminating" type of NDE. It is an irrefutable fact that there has never been, nor will there ever be any two experiences that are identical, since there are no two souls who are identical. No two people have the exact same history. A minority of the cases have very deep core experiences which include encountering the master being of light, having a life review, and receiving universal knowledge.

For the purpose of acquainting the reader with nearly all of the aspects that one might encounter in an illuminating NDE, I shall present an ideal composite. Please keep in mind that it would be rarer than rare to have such a quintessential experience (though a true blessing for sure).

Let us use the example of a gentleman having a massive heart attack that causes a cardiac arrest. He feels severe pain, clutches his chest, slumps over, stops breathing, and becomes unconscious. He "awakens" to find himself floating up out of his body. He looks down on his body and at the people who are working on him such as paramedics, doctors, nurses, relatives, neighbors, or passersby. He may try to communicate with them, trying to tell them that he is here and alive, but they cannot hear him. He may even try to tap someone on the shoulder, but his hand goes straight through. He may even know their unspoken thoughts and may hear them pronouncing him "dead."

Then there is usually described a moment of darkness, following which he finds himself in an enclosure, often described as a tunnel. I have also had it described as a corridor, tube, the inside of a slinky toy, and an igloo-shaped structure, just to name a few variations. A ringing, buzzing, or clicking sound may be audible, or even a whooshing sound, as he is propelled up this tunnel. He realizes that he is not touching the ceiling, floor or sides. He may be accompanied by other beings such as deceased relatives, guides, or angels. Soon he has an awareness of a light at the other end, initially appearing as a tiny sliver. As he gets closer, it becomes bigger and bigger and brighter and brighter, yet it doesn't hurt his eyes. He feels truly drawn toward this light. Remember, when one is out of body one is pure consciousness, in touch with cosmic, or universal, consciousness.

The tunnel ends at a bright, beautiful, warm, loving, spiritual place, often described as a garden. Other descriptions have included a city of light, a pastoral setting, a large waiting room, and a library just to name a few variations. The classic "pearly gates" have also been described.

Everything at the other end of the tunnel is composed of, radiates, and vibrates with that warm, loving light. This incredible light has an essence to it that envelops him with unconditional love. It seems to have a personality that bathes him with compassion and acceptance.

He may be approached by friends or relatives who have gone before. He may see guides, angels, or other beings of light, and all radiate that warm, loving light. There may be described a master being of light, who is named according to his cultural and religious background. Therefore, that being may be called Christ, Allah, or Jehovah, for example. One person called him "Big Guy," and another labeled him "The Man." A gentleman who came up through the '60s crowned him "The Big Kahoona," and a Star Trek "Trekkie" labeled him "Number One." This master being exudes unconditional love, peace, and caring, which is communicated telepathically.

It is usually at about this point in the experience that he may have a flashback or review of his life. This review can take many forms. It can be a three-dimensional panorama, or it can be a quick slide presentation. He may be shown specific fleeting events of his life which may or may not have particular meaning to him, or he may view every second of every day of his entire life to this point in time. He may see, hear, and feel every thought, word, and deed, reexperiencing not only how he felt at that time, but actually feel how the other person felt. This is the ultimate learning experience.

The master being of light, guides, relatives, or other beings that are present may make empathetic comments during the life review. They will suggest to him possible beneficial changes regarding his future thoughts, words, and deeds. The experiencer does not feel he has been judged except for self-judgment. (The LTP experiencers, on the other hand, often feel that they were judged by others than themselves.) The being of light is compassion personified. A few subjects have had reviews of apparent previous lifetimes and a few were shown apparent future lifetimes.

He may describe a place of learning, such as a library, where he may be allowed to see the very large "book of life." He feels a sense of timelessness. On this earth plane we have the time to change our mind about a particular thought, but on the "other side" what one thinks becomes immediately manifest and questions are answered even before they are fully formulated. Therefore, time as we know it here does not exist on the astral plane.

I will digress for a moment and share with you what Wilson said about his life review and the concept of time on the other side:

> The life review was multidimensional. I felt it. I felt the pain and also the joy. You don't get one without the other. I could see the whole thing and it was so totally mindboggling that something like that could happen in microseconds. Your sense of time and space is so distorted. We tend to think of linear time and how long it takes a car to crack up. Well, you know, the action and the whole thing didn't take but five seconds (referring to the impact of his car with a truck that caused the accident and his temporary death). Yet I relived a whole life. To the average person that's impossible. Yes, it is impossible if you're used to using earth terms.
>
> Let me see if I can explain to you the difference in time here on earth and time over there. I had an occasion to do a copy of a series of tapes I had done for TV. I wanted copies of both the video part and the audio part. The guy said we don't have any problem with the audio part 'cause we can just zip them, but the video has to be done in "real time." So if it's twelve hours, then it'll take twelve hours to reproduce it. No kidding! That's the distinction between real time and audio dub time. So when you're applying that to what I went through it makes real sense. Time on the earth is measured in real time, and time over there is like audio dub time. That is how I would explain it to someone who hasn't had one of these experiences.

On the astral plane, "ask and ye shall receive" is the rule with reference to knowledge, so that our subject may become privy to answers to universal questions and be given other divine knowledge. Alas, that information may be "wiped clean" from his memory upon return to his physical body.

Thoughts of unfinished business or thoughts of relatives left behind may bring our gentleman back instantaneously. Often the person wishes to stay with the being of light and with his deceased relatives because he feels he has come "home." He is told, gently but firmly, that he must come back. The specific reason for his return may or may not be apparent. He then feels a "tug" as he is sucked back into his body, or he may simply "lose consciousness" and then "wake up" back in physical form.

When this type of wonderful experience occurs it is usually very transformative, bringing with it significant life-altering changes in attitudes and beliefs. One is usually kinder, more loving and more empathetic, nonjudgmental, treating others according to the Golden Rule, practicing forgiveness and unconditional love, and usually having a thirst for knowledge.

Understandably, many people feel angry upon returning to their physical state, especially if their body is painful and traumatized. Lack of understanding on the part of medical personnel, relatives, friends, and coworkers can further complicate things. I know several experiencers who changed physicians because they no longer felt a rapport when their experience and subsequent personality changes were not acknowledged or understood.

———

One might assume that the longer the cardiac arrest, the deeper and more profound the episode, leading to even more significant life-altering changes. This is not necessarily so.

David was clinically dead for seventy-five minutes. At age thirty-two, he underwent a six-hour operation, after suffering for years with severe ulcerative colitis. His total colon was removed, an ileostomy ("bag") was created, and he was transfused with six units of blood. He developed complications that escalated to a full-blown cardiac arrest. This was obviously such an unusual event (with reference to the resuscitation with full medical recovery after seventy-five minutes) that it was published by his cardiologist in the April 24, 1967 issue of the well-respected *Journal of the American Medical Association*. David experienced the feeling of being covered with a luxurious blanket of velvet while in total blackness. He heard everything that was going on. Despite the fact that he did not meet the being of light or deceased relatives, have a life review, or even traverse the tunnel, he did have very moving permanent changes. The peace, joy, and love that he felt set him on a spiritual path which has continued to this time. He now knows the reason he was allowed to live. His brother and sister-in-law were both killed in a plane crash, leaving their four children to be raised by David and his wife, along with two children of their own.

There are times when a Near-Death Experience may occur to prepare one for a loved one's future death. Marsha was thirty-one years old in 1973 when she had her NDE secondary to drowning. Her youngest of three sons was six at the time. She said:

> I could never in my life explain to you the light, the tranquillity, the beauty. I thank God for allowing me to die. Dying is beautiful. But a few months ago my oldest son was killed, burned in a house fire. The fire marshal said that he was totally burned. They only had a tiny part of his torso where he had made it to the shower and turned on the cold water. They said, though, that his first breath scorched his lungs with temperatures about 3,000 degrees. The autopsy sent word to us that he did not suffer. He died of smoke inhalation, not burns. And I'm at peace because I know from my experience that God gave me when I drowned that it's the

most beautiful feeling. So we have comfort because we know he died instantly, and I have comfort because of my Near-Death Experience. And speaking with you about all of this has healed me even more.

Blissful Childhood Near-Death Experiences

As we shall see, all NDEs may be very transformative, including those which occur during childhood. They often light the way to a lifelong spiritual path. There has been surprisingly very little written about these childhood experiences, especially the Less-Than-Positive ones (which will be discussed in chapter five). I respectfully suggest reading Dr. Melvin Morse's Book, *Closer to the Light,* which is a study exclusively of the NDEs of children.

Childhood NDEs are so very important that the Vol. XVIII, No. 3, 1999 issue of The International Association for Near-Death Studies' publication of *Vital Signs* is devoted to them. Diane Corcoran, Ph.D., president of IANDS, summed up many of the important issues very well. She said:

> Many adults have adjustment issues following their NDE. What do you think happens to children? Many don't understand what happened to them. They try to tell their parents and the parents tell them it was just a dream. They have no place to get information. They were in this wonderful place, with angels and spirits that visited them, then all of a sudden they are jerked away from the angels, and they wonder if they were bad or not worthy of being in heaven with the angels.
>
> They come back from the experience and have light beings or little people surround them and communicate with them. No one else in the family sees or hears these beings, so the other children or family members tease them. They try to tell the teacher about the experience and the teacher tells them to be quiet and not talk about such silly things. They are alone with many questions and no place to get information. . . .
>
> Some children will not even remember the experience, but will have many of the aftereffects and wonder what is wrong

with them. They may have had the experience as an infant, and repressed or forgotten it. However, as they grow up, everybody notices they are different. They have many allergies; they may not like loud noises or bright lights. They are frequently very intuitive, sensitive, affectionate, and have an understanding, vocabulary and insight into things way beyond their years. They may even have some psychic or healing ability. These are all part of the possible aftereffects, yet who will be there to listen to these children and let them know that they are OK? . . . .

These children are different, they will look at life differently and will have valuable information and insight if they are helped to understand their experience and differences. However, if they are laughed at, made fun of, and told that they did not have these experiences, how will this affect their feelings or behaviors? Would we really be surprised to see them become angry, frustrated, or acting out, if no one believes them or pays attention to them? I believe this may be a critical issue with some adolescent behavior today, and that we have underestimated its importance. . . .

How many children are out there having had these experiences—2 million or 20 million? A childhood illness, a near-drowning incident, accident, a fall or an injury are all possibilities where children could have an NDE and not even go to a hospital. . . .

Equally important is what is happening to all the children in hospices, cancer wards and children's hospitals. They are having multiple experiences, some NDEs and some near-death-like experiences, that are frequently missed because the family or health care providers believe it to be confusion, or medication related. These children have precious gifts to share with their parents and siblings. They are gifts that could help the parents over their grief when they lose this child or another loved one. The dying give us such valuable gifts and lessons if we know how to listen. . . . Children are seeing their deceased parents, grandparents, and other departed spiritual beings who have come to help them transition. Often the children are eager to join those on the other side, but they don't know how to tell those left behind they are leaving and that they want to go. There are many important implications for care providers and families if they understand the NDE and what it means to children. . . . Not knowing or not understanding the near-death experience is equivalent to seeing a bleeding child and not knowing enough to bandage the wound. . . . Talk to your kids, listen to their stories—you might be surprised by the information you get.

———————

Adele S. is a lovely lady medical patient of mine. She and I had an instant rapport for a multiplicity of reasons. Perhaps the most important was the fact that we both had profoundly handicapped sons, and lived with the constant fear and anxiety that we would precede our children in death, thereby leaving them on this earth plane without us to care for them.

Adele's son was confined to a wheelchair because of end-stage muscular dystrophy. He had a profound Near-Death Experience which he shared with his mother. In the NDE he "saw" his deceased friend, who said to him: "I've come to get you. I've been here before but you weren't ready to go. You were called back. Now I'll show you where we'll be and soon I'll come back for the last time." With that, they walked through these huge open doors and he saw the blissful magnificence of the heavenly realm. The next day he did, peacefully, go into spirit. You can just imagine the comfort his mother received from his having shared his NDE!

———————

"Babe" had the first of her three NDEs when she was six years old.

> I had my tonsils out on the kitchen table. My father and two neighbors held me down while the doctor gave me the ether. All of a sudden I'm standing at the bottom of these stairs and this man is coming down. I look up and I say: "Jesus!" and He comes down and grabs my hand. I'll never forget His hand or His fingers. They were long, tapered piano fingers, so soft and so warm. Jesus was magnificent! I felt such serenity and peace!

He has a beautiful face, thin, and shoulder-length, soft, sandy-colored hair. His skin is light tan, cream color. Beautiful! As He came down the stairs I saw His toes. He wears sandals, open in the front and back, with a strap around the ankle. It's so vivid in my mind! When your time will come, you'll remember what I said. He said to me: "Don't worry, baby, everything is going to be all right. I'll always be with you."

I woke up screaming: "I saw Jesus! I saw Jesus!" The doctor came running. They sent someone down to the church, and the Mother Superior came to the house. I told them the story and they all had tears running down their cheeks. I grew up loving Him so, always doing the right thing, always behaving, always being good because I knew Jesus was with me. When I talk about it I still cry. I am sixty-eight years old now, and I live with that moment. Those few minutes that I was with Him have guided me my whole life. He has made me the human being I am.

Babe had two subsequent Near-Death Experiences. One occurred during surgery to a blocked carotid artery. She was blessed to encounter Jesus again, as well as her deceased mother and father. The last NDE occurred during vascular bypass surgery.

———————

Helen T., from Seattle, is now fifty-three years old. She had her NDE at eight years of age. She feels that her clairvoyant abilities are a direct result of her experience. She loves children, and has taken care of them for twenty-five years. She said:

I drowned. I was at camp. It was a very crowded pool. There were kids all around me, and I sort of got shoved under water. I tried to get back up but I slipped and fell back in. My body was getting real heavy and then I blacked out. As I was blacking out I felt calm and peaceful. The next thing I knew, I saw myself under water, and I could see everybody in the pool. I thought: "This is strange!"

Then I started going up this tunnel. That's where the little deer met me, at the end of the tunnel. The little deer lead me out of the tunnel and down this black road. Then there was a beautiful garden, absolutely beautiful. There were flowers and just one giant tree. The colors were very bright. I was trying to take it all in, and yet it didn't make sense to me. I sat there looking at everything, and then I saw these seven children in the garden. They were wearing togas, white robes. They were around my age. I saw them from a distance, boys and girls.

Then they saw me and kind of said: "Come on in." I hesitated, but then I thought, "Why not? They look like they're having fun!" Then I was starting to go in and I felt this force pushing me back. It was a really strong force, and as I tried harder, it pushed me back harder. Just before the force pushed me back to my body, I saw what I first thought was an angel. But he was just a man. He was wearing a long, white gown, and he was holding a lamb. He had a long white beard and long white hair. To me he was just an old man, but I knew he was an angel. He told me that if I lead a good, moral life that I have nothing to fear from death.

Then I was back in my body. The lifeguard said: "Thank God you're all right. I must have worked on you for a half hour." For a long time I didn't tell a soul about what happened. Then when I was a teenager I had to say something. My grandmother passed away. It really upset my mother because I think she was really afraid of death, herself. So I told her what happened and then she was no longer afraid.

Amy had two NDEs as a child. She is my medical patient. As is so often the case, I knew the moment I first saw her that she was an experiencer. She is a very talented professional photographer. She said:

I had my first one at three or four years of age. I was swimming in the ocean and the undertow yanked me out to sea. I was an innocent child, twirling and twirling. I was pushed to the bottom of the ocean. This boisterous voice, loud like thunder, said: "Don't struggle." I quit struggling and I swear to you that the ocean spit me out onto the earth again.

The second one happened when I was seven years old. I fell into the pool while everyone was inside the house watching TV. I came up out of my body and was looking at them through the sliding glass door. I saw what they were watching on TV. Then I was back in my body, face down in the pool. There were four angels, no wings, above me. Then I was suddenly in the arms of this man, like a giant, glowing, in white. I could feel the softness of his hair, as soft as spun silk. He had a beard as white as snow. I never felt so much love! He *is* very large, because He *is* everything! He held my face near his and filled me with his grace! He said everything was going to be okay.

Ruth P. lives in Oklahoma. She described her childhood NDE:

I was born December 1, 1928, so on July 4th of 1937 I was nine years old. Being crazy about low-flying airplanes, my cousin, Lois, had me sit on her feet. She kicked me off and I landed on my right arm, causing a double fracture of the elbow. I was taken to the hospital by my dad and Uncle Jess. I was so dirty from playing, that they tried to give me a bath. They were stripping off my clothes in front of Dad, Jess, and the doctor. I kept pulling the covers up! So the doctor decided I had to be put to sleep so they could wash me.

Never a day goes by that I don't think about it, even all these years later. It has always given me the courage to go on in life, because I feel Christ loves me because He let me see Him. Here is what happened. The doctor had an ether cone. He held it up to the light and said: "Ruth, I want you to look into this cone and say your ABCs." Then he put the cone over my face.

Immediately I was in the form of a stick person. I entered into this tunnel from my left. Everybody was in the form of a stick person—women, men, and children, whether they were standing or being held. No one seemed to want me! I was being shoved from one side of the tunnel to the other side. I felt neglected as I always felt in life, because I was always being called the black sheep by my mom. There was a roaring that was so loud that it was as if I was in a vacuum cleaner bag.

There was almost total darkness except for a bright light at the end of the tunnel. As I was being shoved side to side I saw this image, and I knew it had to be Christ. I had never heard of a tunnel or bright light. Christ looked like the pictures you see of Him. He's a handsome man with sharp features. He has sandy-colored hair and a long beard and mustache. He was dressed all in white, like a karate suit, and had on white sandals. He was tall. He even had a white belt tied on the left side. He said nothing, just stood there. Then I got within a few feet of the light. I guess I could have walked into it, but there was this stick man with a long beard and a small stick boy in front of him. He said: "Go back, Ruth. You haven't lived yet." I woke up in recovery. So many, many things have happened to me where I should have been dead but I'm still here. Why?" (My answer to Ruth is that you are a very dear person, and are most certainly not only a blessing to me, but to everyone who meets you!)

Varying Descriptions of the Other Realms

I have often been asked during discussions about Near-Death Experiences, especially by the "naysayers," if I can explain the tremendous variation of descriptions of the other realms. The following is what feels right to me. Let's just say that a being from another planet decides to visit earth, but first wants to speak to earthlings so they can describe it to him. Obviously a person who lives in the Amazon jungle would describe earth one way, a person living the Swiss Alps another way, a person living on the ocean in Fort Lauderdale a third way, a person at the Arctic yet another way, and so forth.

Yet, all of these people absolutely do live on earth. Well, why should we be surprised that there are as many different descriptions of the other realms? Our earth has many very different city architectures, as well as many styles of libraries, homes, and other buildings. Why shouldn't they be as varied in the other dimensions? We have so many different looking people all over this earth, so why wouldn't one encounter different looking beings "there"?

Not Everyone Who is Clinically Dead Has a Near-Death Experience

I propose that not everyone needs to have an NDE (or an LTP). Those who have been on spiritual paths for some time may have already come to the realization that death is not to be feared, and that we are all responsible for every second of our lifetime. They may have already learned, or be on their way to learning, the many other lessons. Occasionally a person may forget that he had an experience. Actually, the majority of NDErs say that, even if fifty years has elapsed since the occurrence, they remember every detail as though it happened yesterday. It is an interesting fact that a few subjects who had multiple incidents have stated that sedating drugs such as anesthesia actually inhibited, rather than promoted, a deep experience.

Now that we are all acquainted with what is meant by the "typical" Near-Death Experience, we will begin our discussion about the Less-Than-Positive (frightening) Experiences.

TWO

The Less-Than-Positive Experience: Overview

A Less-Than-Positive Experience, or LTP, is one which the experiencer interprets in part or whole to be frightening, because it elicits feelings of terror, despair, guilt, and/or overwhelming aloneness.

These frightening experiences have been called "inverted" by Kenneth Ring, a "photographic negative" by Gracia Fay Ellwood, and "distressing" by Dr. Bruce Greyson and Nancy Evans Bush. Unfortunately, most of the other researchers have labeled them as plain "negative." I find the word "negative" to be offensive and false. The LTPs promote such phenomenal learning, self-introspection, and soul growth that the word "negative" is a misnomer. Every LTP experience I have studied has been transforming, but because they are frightening to the person at the time it occurs, I certainly cannot label them "positive" experiences—thus the term "Less-Than-Positive."

In a spiritual sense, we are all in the same boat. Every good thing that we do affects all mankind, and the same is true of all evil.

—Aryeh Kaplan

Frequency of LTPS

My data reveals that 17.7 percent of my study group had an LTP experience. Gallup and Proctor, in *Adventures in Immortality* (McGraw Hill, 1982), found that only 1 percent of the people who had a brush with death "had a sense of hell or torment." Slightly more than 30 percent of this 1 percent also had something positive about their experience, compared with 25 percent of my Less-Than-Positive group.

P. M. H. Atwater, in *Beyond the Light* (Avon, 1994), estimated that approximately 14 percent of her subjects had an "unpleasant and/or Hell-like experience." Kenneth Ring, another prominent researcher, stated in *Heading Toward Omega*: "Most authorities seem agreed that they represent perhaps one percent of all reported cases, perhaps less. In my own experience, having talked to or heard the accounts of many hundreds of NDErs, I have never personally encountered a full-blown, predominantly negative NDE, though I have certainly found some NDEs to have had moments of uncertainty, confusion, or transitory fear." Similarly, Dr. Michael Sabom (*Recollections of Death*, Harper and Row, 1982) and Dr. Raymond Moody (*Life After Life* and *Recollections on Life After Life*, Mockingbird, 1977) did not report any LTP experiences.

An accurate estimate of the frequency of LTPs is difficult to make. Every subject in every study is necessarily self-selected. The person has to be willing to come forward and discuss his experience. Many of the researchers obtained their subjects through ads in publications, specifically requesting people who had had frightening experiences. It is probable that some of those respondents were counted in several studies. That would tend to cause a problem with the accuracy of the estimate. I have verified that my subjects have never been interviewed by any other researcher, nor were their accounts ever placed on the Internet or published anywhere prior to our interview. As a matter of fact, over 20 percent of my subjects (NDEs and LTPs) had never told their story to anyone before, including relatives and friends.

Just as many people who had the "pleasant light" experiences remain hesitant to report them for fear of being ostracized, it is understandable why there is an even greater paucity of LTPs reported. Because the LTPs have been discussed so infrequently, those who have experienced them typically feel that they will be chastised and judged. The popularity of the prototypical light NDEs in the media may also silence the LTP experiencers, who have concern that the public at large will label them as second-class citizens. It is interesting that of the over 300 people whom I interviewed, the only cancellations were those who had had an LTP. Once people realize that they will not be judged by the interviewer or society, I would anticipate that more will come forward.

Cardiologist Maurice Rawlings, in *Beyond Death's Door* (Thomas Nelson, Inc., 1978), stated:

> I have found that an interview immediately after patients are revived reveals as many bad experiences as good ones. . . . It is important to interview people who have died immediately upon resuscitation, while they are still in trouble and calling for help and before the experience can be forgotten or concealed.

I vigorously disagree. I was present at the resuscitation of several of the people in my study. These experiences are so profound, both the typical NDEs and the LTPs, that repression is hardly an option. I have found that until a person is able to work through why an LTP occurred, the experience acts as a thorn in his side. Regardless of the LTP occurring one hour or forty-five years prior to the interview, the experiencer recalled every vivid detail. Less than 5 percent of my more than 300 subjects feel that their memory of the event has decreased in any way. Rawlings neglected to state exactly how many people he interviewed, as well as how many of them were frightening experiences. I do wholeheartedly agree with Kenneth Ring that, "A reading of Rawlings' book shows that it is not really an objective survey of near-death experiences but is essentially a proselytizing Christian tract."

Most researchers on this subject would agree that in God we trust; all others bring data! Interviewing only those people who have been "freshly" resuscitated ignores or misses the significant life-altering changes that take time to evolve. I believe that those life-altering changes, more than anything else, are what validates the LTP experience. The proof is in the pudding, which takes time to cook.

Why Some People Have Less-Than-Positive Experiences

There are three main reasons why a Less-Than-Positive Near-Death Experience may occur. First, it may occur in order to challenge the person to stop, look back, and reevaluate all previous choices, actions, reactions, thoughts, and words, in order to make midcourse changes in direction. Second, an LTP experience may occur if the experiencer has a Less-Than-Positive, less than loving, or fearful mindset just immediately prior to the event. Third, if one grows up with negative programming expecting hell fire and brimstone, then that is what he or she projects to the cosmos and that is what he or she will be given to experience. Near-Death Experience researcher Mally Cox Chapman has suggested that only people with strong egos will remember an LTP experience. Also, it has been suggested that negativity in one's aura (energy field), and/or entities from lower astral planes attached to one's energy field, may facilitate a Less-Than-Positive Near-Death Experience to occur.

It is my opinion that every single one of us could have an LTP. It is a learning tool that forces one to look back and reevaluate a lifetime of choices. Carl Jung wrote about what he referred to as "our shadow," which is where shame lays. We must all own up to our shadow.

Rabbi Harold S. Kushner, author of the best-selling *When Bad Things Happen to Good People* (Avon, 1983), said in *How Good Do We Have to Be?* (Little Brown & Co., 1996) that we are told by society that we have to be perfect, but no one can be perfect. This obviously leads to a lot of conflict when we feel that we cannot live up to society's (or our family's) expectations. I believe that these conflicts and/or our past choices, actions, and reactions that we may deem "unacceptable" lead one to have an LTP instead of a luminous experience.

In their upbringing, many people were programmed with erroneous or incomplete information. The LTP brings this to their attention, as we will see. Some people need a little nudge for one reason or another, and some need the LTP to show them the exit from their pity party. Some people need to realize that the only judging that is real, and that matters, is the judging from within.

Nancy Evans Bush has said: "What we repress and refuse to acknowledge can control us. One of the cosmic laws is that one must do their shadow work. There is no option. The dark experiences are an invitation, not an answer, to go along and find out who we really are while we are still here, not after death." The LTP gives us permission not to be perfect. We are all human, and all human beings make mistakes and poor choices on occasion.

The LTP experience is not an all-purpose tonic for whatever ails us, but it can be the impetus to self-introspection, which will ultimately cause positive changes. We cannot escape ourselves, our past, or our previous choices or actions. We must learn to love and accept ourselves, own up to our previous choices, and then the healing will begin. When we love ourselves, then we can love others.

Kenneth Ring states: "The NDE is, indeed, a healing experience, where a benevolent healing force intrudes itself at the critical moment and provides soul-saving revelation." This can be particularly true with the LTP experience. Dr. Ring calls it the "healing balm of unconditional love and acceptance." I regard the LTP as the most precious gift we could give ourselves, with the help of the cosmic forces, to set us on the path to healing.

––––––––––––

The experience that follows illustrates most of these points.

Wesley was raised in an Episcopalian family. He had his LTP experience in his early twenties, secondary to a drug overdose. His account is particularly fascinating because of the tremendously positive impact it had on his life, and also because he visited both a previous lifetime and a future lifetime. He stated:

> One minute I was laying in my bed, and the next minute I was out of my body in this fog, a graying haze, moving towards a brightness. It was a light that has no definition. I was definitely on a journey through an enclosure without specific walls.
>
> At the end, I was in some great space. I had a nonverbal communication with an entity who was probably a guide. I kept trying to define the entity's shape, in concrete terms, but couldn't. It wasn't a person. I think I asked if the entity was God or Jesus, and the answer was "no." I certainly thought he was a good and all-knowing being.
>
> I was getting answers to questions from that guide, but strangely enough I don't remember most of the answers. One explanation was clear, though. There seemed to be an equality, equal balance, between good and evil. My upbringing had lead me to believe that God was omnipotent, but the answer I got was that one can choose to be in the camp of good or in the camp of evil. Those two forces are constantly at balance with one another, with equal strength and power. I was also given information about a "third eye." I wish I could remember more about that. What is strange, is that even after all these years, if I cross my legs in a certain way I get a strange feeling and remember those words "third eye." (Wesley has never read any metaphysical literature nor studied meditation in this lifetime. He raised the possibility of this being a "carryover" from a previous lifetime.)

I visited at least two different lifetimes, almost like a recollection. I was viewing it like a panorama. One was in an older time and one seemed to be a future time. In the previous lifetime, I was in jeopardy. Someone was after me and I was afraid. I was cowering and crawling on the floor. In the future lifetime, we were involved in some kind of war, shooting one another but not with guns, with light, almost like tracer bullets. It was around that time that the guide said to me: "You are one of the strong," and that was part of what convinced me to come back. You need to understand that even though I wasn't consciously overdosing, I was playing brinksmanship, and it takes courage to admit that you were trying to commit suicide. The entity was helping me in the decision-making process, and it was then that I got serious about recovery. I consciously decided to come back.

Wesley received what he needed from the experience. He was a victim in a previous lifetime, where he saw himself "cowering and crawling on the floor." It was a critical turning point in this lifetime, teaching him that he may choose not to play the victim. He knows that he chooses his own destiny. He chose life. He admittedly made the conscious decision to exit his "pity party." He also learned that one may choose between good and evil. He needed to see himself as a warrior in a future lifetime. That, and the fact that the guide told him that he is "one of the strong," gave him the strength to enter a drug rehabilitation program and then go back to school. Wesley told me that he did not feel judged by the entity or by any other being except himself, and feels that his self-judgment was transforming. He admitted to me that when he "was drugging," he neither "liked nor loved" himself, and felt he "could certainly not love anyone else either." He now "loves and respects" himself, is very happily married, and is the father of two daughters.

I'm proud to say that he has now completed his doctorate in psychology and is doing very well. Wesley did not have a life review of this present lifetime because it wasn't necessary. He knew full well that he had wasted quite a lot of time with his self-destructive behavior. This was his wake-up call—his turning point.

What We See, Hear, and Feel During an LTP Experience

We determine what we see, hear, and feel during an LTP experience! Spoken words and thoughts are energy. We know from NDErs that information is both given and received telepathically (without the mouth moving or sound being produced) on the astral plane. Energy is information. Energy contains information. That is what allows a psychic or medium to do a "reading." Since we know that energy is never totally destroyed, every single previous thought we have ever had becomes a part of universal consciousness and every action of our lifetime becomes a part of cosmic memory. We have all heard the saying that thoughts and words have a life of their own. The cosmic forces know everything about us and know what we "need" to see, hear, or feel to break through our self-protective wall and cause us to reassess past decisions, words, thoughts, and actions. I firmly believe that we, ourselves, determine not only the type of experience we have, but also its content long before it ever occurs. A person having a brief "light" experience may only need to feel the warm fuzzies. The need of the LTP experiencer is usually more complex. William Serdahely, in an article in the *Journal of Near-Death Studies* in 1995, titled "The Individually Tailored Hypothesis" stated: ". . . each NDEr receives what he or she needs during the NDE in a way that the NDEr is able to accept." Wesley's story confirmed this.

Michael Brooks, in *Instant Rapport* (Warner Books, 1989), explains that each of us is primarily either visual, auditory, or kinesthetic. If a person's model of the world is primarily a visual one, then he will see things as pictures, lines, and shapes. If his primary representational system, on the other hand, is auditory, then he hears the world through sounds, tones, and words. If he is primarily a kinesthetic person, he will navigate the world by touch and feelings. Even when one of my subjects didn't realize what his own representational model was, I could usually tell by his choice of words in the interview. Visual and auditory people were the easiest to spot, for obvious reasons. Kinesthetic people used words such as "feelings, exciting, pressure, touch, cold, musty, warm," etc. We will see in the interviews presented here how a person's view of the world may determine the type of LTP that he has. The symbolism, itself, comes from the person's past, his beliefs, and his fears.

Predicting a Less-Than-Positive Experience

I suggest that we can predict an LTP experience, especially knowing the person's unique past and his or her representational model of the world. P. M. H. Atwater stated: "It is almost as if the phenomenon is a particular kind of growth that allows for a 'course correction,' enabling the individual involved to focus on whatever is weak or missing in character development." She further stated: "It has been my experience that whatever we need to awaken the truth of our being will manifest when we need it." For example, I am a totally visual person. I often say: "Do you see what I'm saying?" instead of: "Do you hear what I'm saying?" If I needed to have an LTP as an encouragement to reevaluate my choices, I might well expect (given my unique past and my particular fear) to see snakes. Alternatively, what would also definitely get my attention would be to find myself in total blackness, absolutely void of any visual input. Because I feel secure in small places (and actually feel secure in an MRI machine), rather than feeling bound as many others experience it, I might find myself totally free in vast dark space, with nothing to hold on to and in total fear. That would be my hell. An auditory person might find himself in absolute total silence or, alternatively, might hear very scary sounds. A kinesthetic person might, for example, feel a musty coldness.

————————

Keely is a highly educated lawyer. At the time of her experience she had just turned thirty, was newly divorced, living alone, and completing her law degree. She had always felt that she would never reach thirty, and so she, admittedly, lived very much in the fast track, "burning the candle at three ends," and nearly did self-fulfill that prophecy. She said that at the time she never thought of remarrying or of having children. She stated:

> I was just kind of going week by week, month by month, doin' my thing and that was about where my life was at. I was transiently using cocaine and the near-death occurred during my last usage, which is why it was my last time ever doing drugs. I was by myself, but I don't think I used an inordinate amount. All of a sudden I didn't see anything. It wasn't dark, it was black! I couldn't see even shadows. I couldn't see anything. It was very, very disturbing and very, very uncomfortable. I felt I wasn't in my body. I was detached.
>
> The next thing I remember was a noise in my ears that I'll never forget. It was a loud, humming, high-pitched drone that I heard in both sides of my ears and in my head. It was an internal noise, a very, very bad noise. Then I tried to move, and my body wouldn't move. I felt panicky and I thought to myself: "Well, you did it to yourself and all your life you thought thirty was going to be the number. Well, this is it, so might as well just go." Then I said: "No, I refuse to die. This is bullshit. I am not going to check out." I realized that I wanted tremendously to stay alive.
>
> I did have a flashback, a general negative review of what happened up to that point. I had been on the wrong route for thirty years and I needed to change to a different track. Once I decided that, then I didn't waiver back and forth. I don't remember bargaining with God or anything like that because

I wasn't really a God person then nor am I now. I'm a more spiritual person, but not really a God-bargaining type person. I knew I had to stick around for some purpose. The purpose wasn't to make more money, be famous, or get laid more. None of those thoughts came in. I was to stay for some greater purpose.

Now, all of these years later, I think what's made the difference is that I have my two children and I think that as things go on either they, or whatever they breed, may be the something better that will come out of all of the crap that happened. I didn't necessarily see anything positive coming out of it for me, personally, right when it happened, but I did start to feel like I was part of a bigger plan. It would have been absolutely wrong for me to go against that and be self-centered and slide out.

Reviewing her background, Keely was adopted by loving Jewish parents. She only attended temple services on the High Holy Days and was never Bat Mitzvahed. She said that her mother had tried to commit suicide several times with drug overdoses, and she remembered her being taken out of the house, in that state, many times. She said: "It was a very detached experience. I felt almost nothing about it at the time." She called that her "self-protective mechanism." Keely considers herself to be a very visual and auditory, creative person who was trained in classical music, creative writing, and journalism, as well as law. It is very interesting that she heard that horrible high-pitched droning sound and was in total blackness in her experience. It was certainly a wake-up call. The immediate life-altering result was that she ceased her self-destructive drug use. She said: "Ultimately the experience made an incredible impression on me. It was a real learning experience!"

Different Types of LTP Experiences

Dr. Bruce Greyson and Nancy Evans Bush, in an excellent article published in the February 1992 edition of *Psychiatry*, studied fifty frightening experiences. They then described three distinct types of "distressing Near-Death Experiences." I have categorized my study group's experiences with these types, plus a fourth type I observed.

Type I is an experience almost identical to the "typical" light experience. Instead of feeling peace and joy, the subject feels fear. As the experience progresses, it often turns pleasant. Greyson and Bush described Type II as a "nonexistence or eternal void, sometimes with a sense of despair that life as we know it not only no longer exists, but in fact never did." Type III is described as "graphic and hellish landscapes and entities."

My LTP study data suggests that there is a fourth type, in which the life review is the part of the experience that causes the significant distress or fear for the subject. Whereas in the prototypical NDE nearly every person feels he is judged only by himself, in the Type IV LTP the person often feels he is judged by a higher power that causes an overwhelming feeling of guilt.

Causes of LTPs

There were no specific causes of the LTP experiences that were any different from those that lead up to "typical" NDEs. The most common causes of LTPs in my study were self-induced death (30.6 percent) and physical illness (30.6 percent) which lead to the person's death. Surgery, anaphylactic shock (respiratory and cardiac arrest secondary to a severe allergic reaction), and accidents were other causes.

THREE

Type I LTP: Misinterpreted Pleasant NDEs

The Type I Less-Than-Positive Near-Death Experience is described just the same as the typical NDE, but the person perceives it as frightening. Most of the Type I experiencers had never heard or read about NDEs before their experience. Also, most of my Type I subjects admit that they are used to being in total control of all situations in their lives and confirmed that they felt they were not in control during this event.

Some Examples of Type I LTPs

Lyle is a forty-three-year-old physician. He was raised in a Catholic family, and had not read anything about NDEs prior to his experience. When he was thirty-eight years old he had extensive dental work. After arriving home following the first long appointment, he took the prescribed medication, a type

The body can be thought of as a vessel or a container or apparel which the individual soul puts on. Just as it is natural to throw away a dirty or a worn-out article of clothing and wear a new one, in the same way, you also give up this body and put on a new one. Krishna showed that death was very much like getting rid of an old piece of cloth.

—Sai Baba Gita

he had never taken before. He developed hypotension (very low blood pressure) and a severe allergic reaction which lead to a respiratory arrest. He said:

> I found myself flying through the air, head first, down this dark, dark tunnel. In the distance there was a bright light. I couldn't feel anything. I couldn't feel my body. It was like a numbness. I was in total blackness, pitch black, like the darkest I've ever seen. And it was total emptiness in that tunnel. It was frightening! There was the absence of all noise. I felt totally isolated because of the blackness and the lack of sound. I was consciously trying to fight my way back. I actually was trying to crawl out backwards! My wife gave me mouth-to-mouth resuscitation until the medics got there. I'd say I definitely flirted with death. Afterwards, I did feel very scared and much more vulnerable, and yet I don't fear death.

Lyle admits that he prides himself on being in total control of all situations. He felt that the fear was directly related to his loss of control, which I have found to be the case with several of the LTP experiencers. Because his wife is a nurse who is quite experienced in cardiopulmonary resuscitation, Lyle was brought back from death very rapidly. It was my feeling that if he had stayed a little longer in the tunnel, he would have seen that light become bigger and bigger and brighter and brighter, and then perhaps would have seen his deceased loved ones and felt the unconditional love. This is what most often occurs with the longer Near-Death Experiences.

A high percentage of NDErs experience an initial period of blackness before realizing that they are in an enclosed structure moving forward toward a light. If Lyle had known about these experiences and the initial blackness beforehand, he might not have felt threatened by his lack of control over the situation. Sometimes the circumstances under which the experience occurred cause it to be interpreted as frightening, as will be seen by the next account.

Hilda had her LTP experience twenty-one years ago when she was twenty-nine years old. She was having an arteriogram (a study of the arteries using iodine dye) because the circulation to her arm was being compromised by a rib originating in the neck. She had been told that the dye would be injected into her arm. At the time of the study, however, the doctor insisted on injecting it into the groin. This panicked her because she had previously had surgery on that area. The doctor apparently thought that she was hyperventilating, so he "shoved a paper bag" over her mouth. In reality, Hilda was allergic to the iodine dye and had an anaphylactic (allergic) reaction which led to a seizure and a full cardiac arrest. She couldn't communicate prior to the seizure because of the paper bag being held over her mouth and nose. She said:

> I remember kind of floating off the table and seeing people in white robes and then I saw a tunnel and a bright light. There was someone at the end of that tunnel, but I don't know who it was. It was real foggy and it was like somebody was stopping me from going in. I think what made it so frightening was that I was frightened beforehand. I actually felt myself going, and I heard them say I was going. That frightened me and I was suffocating because of that bag. That didn't help. I tried to tell my doctor about it afterwards, but he said he didn't know what I was talking about. So I stopped talking about it because everyone thought I was crazy. Since no one would talk about it with me, it frightened me more.

Hilda's NDE has many of the features of a peaceful light experience, but she interpreted it as frightening because she heard the hospital staff saying she was dying. This was compounded by the feeling of suffocation. The anxiety increased following her doctor's reaction to her attempt to discuss it. Her great fear going into the experience prevented her from feeling the peace, joy, and love that is usually felt.

I do not mean to imply that everyone who is experiencing fear pre-NDE has a distressing experience. Quite the contrary. I studied two people who were viciously attacked, murdered, and then resuscitated. (One was strangled and the other was stabbed.) Both had very profound luminous experiences. Here's another Type I LTP.

Sixty-two-year-old Dorrie is now a medical secretary. She was raised in a Catholic family and was eight years old when she had an abscessed mastoid lanced on the kitchen table at home. (Doctors often treated patients at home in the 1930s.) Ether was the anesthetizing agent. She remembers it clearly, even though it happened fifty-four years ago.

> **The doctor gave me ether through a strainer. I had this sensation of buzzing in my head and I was going through this dark tunnel. It was like looking through a funnel. I was floating and I thought there was water in the tunnel, so I started to think it might be a sewer. I was being propelled over the water. I felt totally out of control. I felt fear, only fear. Real fear.**

This experience was aborted rapidly because the doctor knew she was in trouble. Ether was a common anesthetic agent used in the 1930s. Sophisticated means of monitoring for possible complications was unavailable. Needless to say, that experience happened to Dorrie many years before she had grown spiritually, and many years before NDEs were acknowledged, described, and discussed, so she had no frame of reference. She was certainly frightened to be in a "dirty sewer." She continued to have fear whenever she thought about ever needing surgery of any type. Since she became my medical patient in Florida we have discussed her experience at great length; she has attended several South Florida IANDS meetings and now has no fear.

Anthony, an eighty-year-old Italian gentleman, also had a Type I LTP experience. This not only demonstrates how our upbringing can continue to influence us throughout our life, but it also confirms the very positive and life-prolonging difference that medical personnel can make if they will listen to their patients. Dan Taylor, a wonderful, caring, skilled CCU nurse at Holy Cross Hospital, called me about a patient who had "coded" (meaning he was clinically dead) and was resuscitated. The Type I LTP experience petrified the patient so, that he was refusing to have the coronary artery bypass surgery scheduled for the next day, which he needed desperately. Dan asked me to come and speak with the patient, which I did after getting permission from both the attending cardiologist and the cardiovascular surgeon. Anthony described his experience:

> I was laying here and felt this pain coming on. Then the first thing I know, I had no pain and I passed out. I saw this big cave and it was filled with white clouds. I felt myself starting to fall down through that cave. I was reaching out to the sides, trying to grab something, and I couldn't. I shouted out for someone to help me. I said: "I'm falling and there's no one to help me!" So I fell down, rather floated down, through there and the next thing I knew there were two nice nurses, one on either side of me saying: "You're gonna make it. We got you back!"

I spent quite a long time with Anthony because he was so very frightened. Why? It certainly was a Type I LTP experience. He didn't know anything at all about NDEs, so he didn't know the light was probably coming! Also, I would have to say (having been married for twenty-five years to a Sicilian gentleman, who was not only tough, but the best of the best) that most Italian gentlemen are used to being in total control at all times. In this experience Anthony was not in control. He admitted that he felt helpless because he was falling, couldn't control his fall, and had nothing to hold on to. And, perhaps more importantly, he was programmed throughout his whole life to assume that anything in a downward direction was "toward hell." So he assumed that he was going to that "fiery bad place." He came to understand that had he not been resuscitated so rapidly, he might well have been enveloped by the loving light at the end of the "cave," and might have been met by his loving deceased wife. He lost his fear and agreed to the surgery. He did fabulously well, and is still doing very, very well!

Nearly all of the Type I LTP experiencers whom I have interviewed prove that one person's trauma may be another person's treasure. None of my Type I LTP subjects had ever read or heard about them until after the fact. Most NDEs would not have been interpreted as frightening, had the person ever heard about them before. Since they had not, it was basically the feeling of not being in control of the situation that caused the anxiety. They didn't know the light was coming! As more and more people become aware of NDEs, this type of LTP may decrease in frequency. As Greyson and Bush suggest, and I concur, the Type I LTP may be regarded as a "variant of the prototypical Near-Death Experience." In the next chapter we will discuss Type II LTP experiences.

FOUR

Type II LTP: The Eternal Void

In the Type II Less-Than-Positive Near-Death Experience, as described by Greyson and Bush, the subject finds him- or herself in a dark void, often feeling restrained, with an overwhelming feeling of aloneness and despair. Mechanistic presences and other shadowy entities have been described.

Twenty-eight percent of my LTP study group had a Type II experience; 50 percent of them called out to God for help; 54.5 percent had self-induced their brush with death, either intentionally or nonintentionally, through self-destructive behavior; 30 percent experienced a life review. None of the Type IIs progressed to a light experience, but several of the Type-II group progressed to a Type III LTP, containing hellish imagery. In the Type II group, 37.5 percent were Catholic, 37.5 percent were Jewish, 12.5 percent were Protestant, and 12.5 percent were members of other religions.

As far as God is concerned, if you have sacred thoughts and engage in good works and good words, then even if you are an atheist you will be dear to Him.

—Sai Baba Gita

It should be kept in mind that most typical NDE experiences do begin as a moment of darkness. It is always possible that if the person was in the experience longer, he might have eventually been bathed in the light. Sometimes the cardiac arrest is reversed almost immediately if medical personnel and equipment are on hand. Bevy Jaegers has suggested in an article titled: "The Black Hole Phenomenon," published in the Spring 1996 *Vital Signs*, that the blackness may be merely the opening of the tunnel.

Jay was thirty-six years old at the time of his episode. He was raised in a Jewish home and moved to Las Vegas to work on a newspaper. He loved the bright lights; the fast, busy lifestyle; the constant sensory stimulation; and always being with people. He admitted "being into gambling and drugs" and was at a party "doing drugs." He stated:

> I think somebody slipped me some PCP and I don't know what everything else was laced with. I died. I left my body and went into an outer darkness and it was eternity. It was a void, incredibly painful. It felt like forever. I know what the meaning of hell is, because it was hell. I was in hell! It was the absence of everything: the absence of love and emotions, just an absolute emptiness. I will never forget the pain. It wasn't physical at all. That's what was so terrifying. It was emotional, psychological, and spiritual pain. My spirit had descended into this place. I was convinced that I was never coming back.
>
> I saw my life somewhere along the way. It was very brief. I felt the whole thing was a judgment. I saw it as a warning. I cried up to God and it was by the power of God and the mercy of God that I was permitted to come back. It was just so intense!
>
> I think God is in control of everything that happens. I think it was a warning from God saying: "You are going to wind up here," meaning if I do anything to myself. No matter

how bad it is here, it can't compare to there. Death is a lot worse than life if you don't help God.

I think what happened was a blessing in disguise. I've stopped drugs, moved back to Florida, and now I'm in Bible college. I used to have a casual attitude about death, but now I actually fear it more. Life on earth is very brief, but eternity is forever. So, yes, it was a warning. I was permitted another chance to change my behavior on earth. I've taken the fear of death and given it to the scriptures. But everyone should know that there is no finality with death.

Jay's experience caused him to change his behavior. The void, with total lack of sensory stimulation, was almost predictable given his busy sensory-packed lifestyle. He is a kinesthetic person. The brief life review made him reevaluate his choices. Fear of death, which commonly decreases or totally vanishes for the light Near-Death Experiencers, is often present or even increased with some of the LTP subjects.

––––––––––

As I said previously, I believe that the cosmic forces know our every thought and hear our every word. They facilitate just exactly what we need to see, hear, or feel to bring about necessary changes in our behavior or thought patterns.

Selma felt just exactly what she needed to feel, nothing more and nothing less. She was twenty-seven years old at the time of her LTP experience. She said:

I used to get very emotional and upset. My favorite phrase was: "I wish I was dead. I wish I was dead." When it happened, the room was so bright that it was brighter than an operating room, white bright. I couldn't move, not an arm, not a leg. I couldn't speak or yell, and I was scared to death. All I can say is that I never wished I was dead again, and that was eighteen years ago. Someone was trying to tell me that if you want to be dead, then this is how it is.

Bottom line for Selma was that suicide is not an option. That is a very frequent theme among the LTP experiences, especially Types II and III.

———————

Anthony was a fire medic for nearly ten years before becoming a policeman. As a fire medic, he was involved in every imaginable type of emergency rescue. This often necessitated starting intravenous lines and doing resuscitations on victims whose medical history was not known. All emergency response personnel live with the daily fear of contracting disease while working under these conditions. When Anthony was diagnosed as HIV-positive at age thirty-six, after being accidentally stuck with a needle during a resuscitation, he became so despondent that he attempted suicide. In his words:

> I had taken a quantity of sleeping pills. I was taken to the hospital and they were working on me. I was deeply unconscious. I felt like my body was floating in darkness, the darkest black I've ever seen. It was like you took somebody's body and just put it up in space. I felt bound up, tied up, but I don't remember any specific wire or cloth or tape or anything like that. I couldn't move or do anything to free myself. I couldn't see anything. It was terrifying! I heard very annoying sounds in my ears, like a siren or horn-type thing constantly going bomp, bomp, bomp. It was very annoying and I couldn't stop it. I thought to myself: "I'm in hell and I can't get out! I'm trapped here!"
>
> Then I heard a voice and I knew it was God. It was weird. The voice wasn't real authoritative, but it was sort of peaceful and calm. He said to me: "If this is what you're going to do, then this is where you're going to be." I perceived it as being in hell, even though I didn't see any little devils or pitchforks or flames. It was terrifying, being suspended in darkness with these annoying sounds. Then I was thinking, but didn't say to God, although He must have heard me: "It's too late, I'm already dead." I said that because I saw them going to cover my

body on the stretcher with a sheet. Then, suddenly, it was like everything just disappeared and I was back in my body feeling calmness, like a relief. It was like I was given the will to live. God was showing me that if you commit suicide, then you'll go to hell. God gave me the choice to either give up or fight.

Anthony's view of the world has always been primarily auditory. As a child, he most remembers the excitement he felt hearing police and fire sirens, and this continued into adulthood when he became a fire medic and later a policeman. He admitted that what he had always thought would be his hell was exactly what he experienced. He was raised in a Catholic home, knowing that "suicide is wrong." The experience confirmed this. He has undergone tremendous life-altering changes as a direct result. He stated: "I know God has a plan for me. It's to help other people who have HIV, and now I have a wonderful wife and son." Anthony has indeed, come to terms with the HIV and is involved in teaching HIV prevention techniques in the work place. He now feels no bitterness.

Franz was a very successful entertainer on two U.S. coasts and in Rome. He was raised Catholic, and while in Rome he often went to the Vatican. He feels that his spirituality was re-awakened there. In 1971, at thirty years of age, he came back to the U.S. "to the night-club scene to perform." He said that one night he and a lady friend were "soused out with scotch." While he was driving, speeding, he ran the car off the road, hit a fence, hit the windshield with his head, and was thrown out of the car. He had a concussion, punctured lung, and fractured ribs. He was out of his body, looking down on the scene when he heard a policeman say: "I wouldn't give you ten cents for his life."

Then suddenly I was in a dark place, going up very, very fast. I kept ascending. I had a great fear in that darkness. I knew I

was coming from a bad place: drinks, drugs, and the entertainment field. I had a short life review. I saw myself as a child
and again in Rome. I cried out to Jesus: "I'm not in a state of
grace, Jesus, let me live and I'll do it right." Then the dark,
dark blackness became dark lavender and then I felt a sudden
sublime serenity, a calmness like I've never felt before, not
even in Rome. I felt He was there, and angels, too, a definite
spiritual presence.

Franz describes himself as primarily a visual person. His whole
adult life was one of bright lights in the entertainment field. The
darkness of the NDE and then the visual life review were what got
his attention and caused him to reevaluate his choice of life-style and
actions. Franz is also a good example (as are most LTP experiencers)
of heightened religiosity after a brush with death. Referring specifically to his life review, he said:

I guess I was shown the innocence of a child and Rome
because I was so peaceful there and I had metaphysical experiences there. I guess I had to get in touch with that again
because I was going back to my old ways. I was being shown
that I had to shape up or ship out, one or the other. In other
words, "get your act together," and I did just that.

My life changed like night and day. I went from living in
top hotels to one room in the Village (Manhattan), where I
was able to get involved in the university of the streets. I
totally changed my career. I've gotten back to my religion and
I've found a church where I feel comfortable. I used to be a
wild man and would fight all the time. I'm much calmer now.
I don't fear death. I'm fearless because I know that if I ask, I
can live again. I know there's a life after life. I know there is
reincarnation.

Franz is now a hypnotherapist.

Shandra is another very visual person who had a Type II LTP experience. She had four of them, in fact, all in her twenties. She was used to a fast, glamorous type of life as a makeup artist for TV and movies. It took her four times to finally "get the message," after which she entered and completed a drug rehab program. In her own words:

> I grew up in a really rich Jewish family on the north shore of Long Island in a big mansion with a dysfunctional, bipolar father. He hit me abusively. The first time I took a drug I was home. I took it to be out of pain. It went on from there. I grew up very angry.
>
> I swallowed a bottle of 100 Quaaludes in California and I remember just fading and hearing people call my family to tell them I was dead. I'm on this steel table in a dark room at USC Medical Center in LA. I just remember looking down from above at this humongous black nurse. She was basically like yelling at my body saying: "You stupid girl!" I know I actually saw my family, even though I was in California and they were in New York. So I traveled that far without my body.
>
> I didn't want to die, but I didn't not want to die. I was in some holding place that was dark, with just a ray of light. There were shadowy figures, and I heard music, definitely angelic music, that had a semi-Christian tinge to it. The entities were telling me: "You have to go back." The message was: "You have a purpose and lessons to learn in this lifetime." I was getting spoken to and getting coached on coming back. I was told I had to find the answers out for myself. See, I wasn't given information. I wasn't open to it because there was so much pain in me. I thought I wanted to die, or at least I didn't want to be in pain, and I didn't know how not to be. All four times I was in that same holding place.
>
> Like I said, I was brought up in a Jewish home and was taught that when you die you just go to sleep forever, which to me was a good comfort, because I didn't want to have to deal with anything. But now I know that if you commit suicide

you don't just go to sleep, but you have to do it again. You have to learn your lessons.

Shandra, as most of the LTP experiencers, proved to have tremendous insight into the "why" it happened, as well as insight into the symbolism.

> That sliver of light was perfect with the darkness, because it was saying to me: "You can get out of here." In other words, just do it!! Do it!! To me, hell is separation from God and we do that to ourselves. I think if you believe in hell, then you'll be in it. Even though it was mostly dark, I felt safe where I was, but the message was to get out because you don't belong here. So I got exactly what I needed and I think that's how it works. After the fourth one I finally got the message and went into a drug rehab program in Florida. It was the stepping stone for me to do some housecleaning. I was twenty-four, knew I had to get off drugs, and when I did get clean I spent seven years in Florida dedicating my life to working with teenagers on drugs and their families. The best thing of all was I married the man who was program director.
>
> Please tell everyone, Doc, that the answer to everything is love. We have to stop accepting negativity, violence, and hostility in the world. Back then I just wasn't getting it. I wasn't understanding. Now I do get it and I don't have to have a Near-Death Experience.

Dennis is a recovering alcoholic. Twelve years ago, when he was thirty-five years old, he was getting "sicker and sicker . . . went into detox," developed a 105-degree temperature, and had to be hospitalized for a ruptured appendix. It was then that he had the experience that changed his life. He said:

> I was going in and out of coma. At one point I was in so much pain from the surgery, staples, drains, and tubes that it was hard to keep fighting. I couldn't communicate. I was

laying on the bed and all of a sudden I was removed from myself. I was up on the ceiling looking down on this thin, frail body, and for the first time I realized how sick I was. Then the room started getting darker and darker. It was like a void of life. It was an absence of light.

I felt bound in the darkness, like a weight was holding me down. It was what I grew up to know as hell. Right before the total darkness, I reviewed my life. For the most part it was things that I was disappointed in myself about. It was like a fast-forward of scenes. I got the sense that it wasn't the particular scenes that were important, but what was important was that I felt it was just so much of a waste. Like wow, there's nothing there! Then I saw these black fragments that started to move. I realized they were silhouettes, shadows of people, and I could hear chains being pulled. I heard moans and I got terrified.

I thought they were my ancestors coming for me, and I didn't want to go. In the middle of all this was a little flicker of light, like a small birthday candle light. Something told me not to look at the darkness, but to just keep looking at the light. And I said: "God, I'm ready to go if you want me, but I've lead such a useless life I'd like another chance to put it right," and just at that point a sword came up through the candle, through the flicker of light, and the whole room lit up. I dropped back into my body and could hear the doctors and nurses saying: "He's alive!"

Dennis was raised Catholic. He said:

I fell away from the Church at about twelve or thirteen. I have found my faith again now through Alcoholics Anonymous. Since my death experience I've returned to the Church, but it's not the same. I go to a Catholic Church, but it's like a Catholic Pentecostal type, a Charismatic type. That's what I like about it. It's a life and spirit. I see myself as a Christian now. That's been a gradual involvement. I don't really see myself as a Catholic, but really as a Christian who has found a

home in the Catholic Church. Sometimes I have difficulty
with people in the Church because they tell me what they've
read and what they've known. I can't quote the scriptures, but
I can tell you how the Lord has touched me.

Dennis said that he felt that the LTP "needed to happen." He
came to his own conclusion that he had wasted his life, but now does
have a purpose for living. That purpose is to share his experience
with people in AA who need to hear it. He said:

The feeling I got was redemption. Hell was the place I was
bound for, but not a place that I have to go now. I had a
choice. I think that was the key to it. It was when I asked God
what I did that I made the choice, and the choice is there for
all of us, all the time. I feel that I'm an emissary of sorts.
When I think someone has tried walking toward the light but
now they're blocked, I'll tell them the story. I know I wasn't
supposed to hoard this experience to myself. It was for other
people, too.

When I asked Dennis why he thinks that we are here, his answer
was: "to reach a oneness with one another and with God. When
we're at oneness with one another, then God is present." Dennis is
working full-time as a maintenance technician and is not drinking.
He, too, got what he needed in the LTP to make necessary changes.

The following episode is presented for two reasons. First, it is very
descriptive of the vortex which is often mentioned in the Type II
experiences and second, the subject's husband, who was very much
alive at the time, was present in the experience.

Carline was twenty-nine years old in 1979 when the incident
occurred. She describes herself as a "very visual and feeling-type person." She was a journalist who used "word pictures" in her writing.
She was in a very stressful marriage, and was five months pregnant at
the time. She had an LTP experience that turned into a beautiful,

light experience. Even though she was pregnant, she had to have emergency surgery for an appendicitis. After being home for a week, she developed severe abdominal pain and had a second operation for a gangrenous intestine. The physiological stress put her into premature labor and the baby lived only four hours. Because of a staph infection, she had yet another operation. She stated:

> This time I was morally, emotionally, and physically absolutely wasted. First it was all black and there was just this bright white light way out, almost like a moon in a black sky up in the left hand corner of the operating room. It started coming down toward me, and as it got closer I could see it was like a swirling vortex. I felt cold and wind. Around the vortex were these faces, just heads. Some I knew, and some I didn't. They were saying: "Come with us. Come with us." The faces didn't look evil and they weren't the faces of the devil, but they were cunning and manipulative, smiling, and I knew I couldn't trust them. I was really afraid at one point that I was going to be sucked into the vortex and that I didn't have control. I was really fighting it. It was nasty.
>
> As the faces were getting closer, I started to recognize that one was my then-present husband's face, and he was telling me to come with them. And I'm thinking, looking at his face: "What are you doing? You're betraying me!" I fought it! Then I got rid of what I considered to be the negative vision, which scared the shit out of me.
>
> It was instantaneous, like a blink! I was terrified and resisting at one point, then like an edit—cut frame—right to the next scene, which was completely different. There was no transition. It was very abrupt. There was a bright light, a beautiful blue sky, and a green meadow with little blue flowers. I stayed there amidst that bright light until I was back in the operating room. The light in the first part of the experience, with the vortex, was very harsh, unfriendly, and judgmental, although it had soft edges. The light in the meadow was warm and all-encompassing, like a soft veil of light.

Why did Carline have the experience and see what she saw and feel what she felt? She told me that it was both preparatory and strengthening. She felt it was a premonition of things to come. It taught her that if she could survive that, then she could survive anything. It reaffirmed her ability not to give up. And, in fact, years later she had many things that she had to fight to survive, including breast cancer. Instead of a "poor-me attitude," she says that her attitude has been: "Okay, now what do we do? What's the next step?"

Carline said that the experience did change her attitude toward her husband. She was leery about him from that point on, and it turned out that he did betray her and they ended up being divorced. She felt it was inevitable. They had a son while they were still married, and when the son was six months old her husband began "doing drugs and drinking and all sorts of stuff. I was disappointed, but not surprised. I was able to pack up my son, move to Florida, and start a whole new life," prepared, she felt, by the experience.

She felt the second part of the experience was "sort of a reward. I made it. It's like I got past the temptation, past the weakness, past the fear and that was my reward for hanging in there." Did she think the blackness and the vortex was hell? She said: "Hell isn't a physical place. It's in your mind. Hell can be right here on earth."

What was the bottom line for Carline?

> It was my turning point, as far as my maturity goes. I was still a kid when it happened, but that was the beginning of a new era for me. I had been the most anal-retentive person you ever met, home at lunchtime dusting and vacuuming every day. Now I don't let little things get to me.

One last example of the Type II LTP occurred to Rochelle, who is an epileptic. Her seizures began when she was fourteen years old, then increased in frequency in her twenties. She said that: "Some of them were really dangerous. One time I had one when I was diving into a pool. I had one in midair and when I hit the water my friends thought I was doing the dead man's float. I had stopped breathing!"

When she was fifty-five years old she was hospitalized with status epilepticus (repeated convulsions, one after the other). She said:

> I was in a place of emptiness, total emptiness. There was no feeling. There was no purpose for anything. My life was meaningless. My taking care of my house, my decorating, and so forth, all had no purpose. I expected the Lord to be there, but He wasn't. There was no God. The experience really scared me because I started to think that maybe there isn't anything after death after all. Maybe we just conjure that up, and maybe my belief in the Lord and this fire that I felt, and the things I thought the Lord had pulled me out of in the past, was just a thing in my mind. Maybe all the miracles weren't miracles. Maybe there really is nothing there. I called on God and He wasn't there. That's what scared me.

I explained to Rochelle that I believe with all my heart that had she not been resuscitated as rapidly as she was, she soon would have experienced the white God light and a wonderful peaceful experience would have unfolded.

As Greyson and Bush stated with reference to the Type II LTP experience: "Individuals in this group are often left not only with feelings of terror, as with other distressing experiences, but also with a persisting sense of emptiness and despair." I agree, and that is why it is often advisable to use the LTP experience as a jump-off point in therapy, to get down to the nitty-gritty and deal with the reasons why it happened. The reasons are all within us, waiting to be confronted.

FIVE

Type III LTP:
The Hellish NDE

The Type III Less-Than-Positive Near-Death Experience, as described by Grey-son and Bush, contains "graphic hellish landscapes and entities." This type comprised the largest percentage, 41.7 percent, of my sample. Greyson and Bush stated that this type does not appear to convert to a peaceful experience with time, but my findings suggest otherwise. We must remember that all of these statistics are dependent on who is willing to come forward and discuss their episode; 13.3 percent of my Type III LTPs began as a peaceful experience and then progressed to one with devilish imagery; 46.7 percent began as a Type III LTP and then transformed into a peaceful experience. Only 18 percent of my Type III LTP subjects had self-induced their death, as compared with 54.5 percent of the Type II group that we just discussed in chapter four. Twenty percent of

*To appreciate heaven well,
'Tis good for a man to have some fifteen minutes of hell.*

—William
McKendree
Carleton

the Type III experiencers had a life review. Loud, often piercing, annoying sounds are common with this group, and it is only in this group that references were made to frightening animals.

The breakdown of the religious background of the Type III LTP experiencers is as follows: 27.8 percent were agnostic or atheistic, 27.7 percent were Catholic, 16.6 percent were Jewish, 5.5 percent Protestant, 5.5 percent Methodist, 5.5 percent Episcopalian, and 11.4 percent were of other religions including Baptist and Pentecostal.

Many Type III experiencers drew conclusions about their episode on their own. Some seemed to feel the experience occurred because they had not believed in God, which changed in every instance after the episode. Several thought that their episode was a result of being "brought up in a Holy Roller religious family where hell fire and brimstone is a constant threat." Many who had attempted suicide felt they had the experience because they had "committed a moral sin."

Examples of the Type III LTP

Rochelle first had the Type II experience presented in the last chapter. Unfortunately, several years later she tried to commit suicide and it was then that she had the Type III experience. In her words:

> I tried suicide twice. The first time was an overdose and I was in the hospital for a month, but I didn't have an experience. Then I did it again. This time I turned the gas on. Up north they have those old radiators. Well, I was in a state of depression and I couldn't stop crying. I couldn't sleep to get away from it. At the time I was not a believer. I didn't believe there was anything after you died. I was agnostic. I didn't believe there was a devil or a heaven or hell. So I thought the only way to get rid of this pain was to end it all. I sealed up the windows and the door, turned on the gas, and I laid down on the bed and went right off to sleep.
>
> Well, all of a sudden I was in this dark place, blackness, total blackness. No light, just a black void. I knew in my mind

I was dead, but I took the pain with me. All the pain I was suffering I took with me. So I thought: "Oh, my goodness, I'm going to have to go through this for an eternity!" Then something touched me on the shoulder, and I looked around and here's this big gorilla, or this ape. Now, for some reason, I associated this ape with Satan. I knew I had died and was in hell and would have to suffer like this for eternity, with this heartache I had, and this pain. I screamed from the pits of my soul. I screamed out for God and I screamed and kept scream- ing. Finally, He pulled me up and BOOM, I woke up! It was three or four hours later, there was gas all over this three-story house, but I wasn't even nauseated. It was like God was say- ing: "Look, I've had enough of this foolishness. There is some- thing after this life," and He showed it to me and He pulled me out of it.

I would like people who are in the position I was in (mean- ing the depression) to know that if they think they're going to escape it by dying, I would like to tell them: no you won't! If you die you'll still have to live in that pain, because you don't really die, so it doesn't do anything. You can't escape it, so don't try to kill yourself. You're gonna' have to work your way through this and you CAN work your way through it with help. There is help out there.

Rochelle, a decorator, is a very visual person. Although her Type II experience did "impress" her, she admits that she wasn't "totally get- ting it." Because she didn't, the experience following the second sui- cide attempt was more graphic and more symbolic. Why the gorilla? Rochelle feels it was because she grew up in the era of King Kong, and was indeed afraid of gorillas earlier in her life.

Rochelle feels that if she'd had the therapy that she needed to treat the depression, then the suicide attempt would not have occurred and the LTP would have been unnecessary. She feels the suicide attempt was absolutely the reason for the LTP because she acknowl- edges that it is morally wrong to take one's life. She now no longer considers herself agnostic, and a most significant life-altering change is that she now choreographs Christian dances and has a ministry of interpretive dance.

———————

Del is another person who admits that he "just wasn't getting the message" with his earlier episodes (Type II LTPs). In other words, he neglected to stop his self-destructive behavior and so it became "necessary" for him to have a Type III experience. I interviewed Del at age forty, as he was entering a drug rehabilitation program for the first time in his life. Here's how he described the first episode:

> It's easy to remember the first one. I was about twenty-three years old. That first one was real profound, but I got used to them after a while. I had been using Demerol IV and I'd overdosed accidentally. The last thing I remember was that I was at a friend's house, and the next thing I knew I "came to" just for a few seconds in the emergency room and everyone was running around. I was in four points (leather restraints) and tied down. They were cutting my clothes off.
>
> I was really scared, but then it got to a point where it wasn't scary any more. It was just real dark, but it was like real peaceful and I knew that dying wasn't scary, except that it just wasn't my time to die because I woke up two days later on life support. It was so peaceful that for a long time I wasn't afraid to die, but that worked against me as you'll find out as I tell you what happened.
>
> I pushed the edge all the time. I pushed to the limit with my drugs. It caused me to overdose several times a year. I'd start convulsing and losing my urine and say: "Well, here I am; here I am again!" I'm fixin' to go for a ride and I'd just let go, and the next thing I'd know several days would have passed and I'd be on life support again. Most of the times it was just an empty darkness, but real peaceful, nothing to be afraid of. I never saw or heard anything. I started reading books and listening to television about people who had said

they'd seen a bright light. I couldn't understand why I hadn't. I could remember one time thinking to myself: "I'm crazy," because I'd been on life support ten times in one year. I was so close to death that I got used to it. I got used to death! I got familiar with death, and it didn't scare me anymore. That's strange! It made me feel almost invincible.

Those were Del's early experiences. Because they gave him a feeling of peace, he was not motivated to stop his drug use. Death had become comfortable and peaceful. The last death experience, a Type III, was a totally different story. He said:

The last one happened about two months ago and it scared me enough to make me come in here for treatment. It started out as blackness, just like the others, but instead of being peaceful, it gave me terrible fear. First I felt bound, and like there was something trying to get in me. I couldn't scream, knew I wasn't dreaming, and couldn't move. Then I saw these people, like a devil worship thing. There was a long spiral staircase with people all the way down, and candles on the side. It was three stories high. There was a guy with tattoos all over at the bottom of the staircase. He didn't have a shirt on. I was fixated looking at those tattoos. As he started saying something about a dog, here comes this big—I mean big—dog. The people on the staircase were saying things, too, and their mouths weren't moving either. I wasn't afraid. I was terrified! Stuff would seem to appear and disappear. It looked like there were goblins up in the trees. It was a trip! I thought: "Now I've had it!" and then I started fighting for my life.

I questioned Del about his past (including the years prior to his drug use) in an effort to determine the reason for the particular imagery. We discussed his religious background, upbringing, family, etc. When he was a teenager, he came from Tennessee to Florida for the summer to work. He stated:

There was a time some people were trying to kill me. It was a bad time in my life. I was out in the street and a bunch of devil worshippers got after me and they were going to kill me. They knew no one would miss me, because they saw me working in day labors. They'd just dump the body in the Glades. It happens there all the time. But something gave me the strength to run from those thirty or forty people for six hours straight! Maybe I could've plucked them off, one by one, because I had a knife, but something stopped me from trying that. I was praying "Oh, please, God" the whole time. The main thing that convinced me that there is a God was this: I had been running for hours, and something just possessed me to stop. I stopped, looked back, and there was one of them just thirty or forty feet away with a bow and arrow. I could see the arrow coming right for my face, and about three feet away it 90'd up right over my head! I mean, that just doesn't happen! It made a ninety degree turn up over my head and then I just took off running again. That made a believer out of me. I saw it! I saw miracles! I never came back to Florida until now, to start the treatment program.

I presented this case with the extra details to make a point. I feel that one sees what one needs to see, hears what one needs to hear, and feels what one needs to feel in order to stop, look back, and re-evaluate those previous choices in order to make necessary changes. In this instance, Del's initial multiple NDEs had him in darkness, but in peace. As in a previous example, I felt that if Del had not been resuscitated as fast as he was then he would have found himself in the tunnel moving toward the light, and possibly would have felt the unconditional love. However, he kept at his self-destructive behavior, self-medicating with drugs, and, at his own admission, felt it was "okay to flirt with death" because he had come to view death as his "partner."

What was the bottom line? He wasn't getting it! Perhaps the Higher Power, Cosmic Forces, Universal Consciousness, or whatever term you would like to use, caused a change in the type of death experience. The imagery from the frightening experience he had as a teenager in the Glades, in Florida, was required to hit the necessary point home. Remember, we had said that words and thoughts are energy, which has become a part of cosmic memory. So the cosmic forces on the other side knew exactly what Del needed to make him stop and review his actions and beliefs in this lifetime. It certainly did shake him into reassessing his life.

I agree with Dr. Melvin Morse when he says, in *Transformed By the Light,* that the transformative element in the transcendental Near-Death Experience is the light, but now I believe that when one looks at the Less-Than-Positive Near-Death Experiences, the *absence* of the light causes transformation in that person's life. When I asked Del if he had experienced a life review, he said:

> Yes, one of the last times, and I think that's why I'm afraid. Everything's changed the last few times. The review of my life happened so quick, I can just remember being afraid and seeing it all going so fast and just going away. There it goes, there it goes, there it goes. You know how you can hold up a deck of cards and flip through them real fast with your finger? It was like that, real fast. I just remember feeling bad, knowing this time is different. It was going so fast I really couldn't grasp everything I was seeing, but I knew it was me. It was like my life was just goin' away, real quick. I can't remember one particular thing. What was scary was: this is it! This is the end! I remember thinking I was being shown that because now it's over. The forty years is over. You get a quick look and then that's it. It wasn't that peaceful feeling at all. So when I didn't die, I thought: "Well, I'd better do something different." I don't want to have a violent death.

It was very significant that Del was shown a life review. He said that he felt he was supposed to really look at every single day so that he would understand how quickly it can be over. He said that he felt a lot of judgment, but that it was from himself, rather than from without. As of the writing of this book, he has remained off drugs and is working steadily.

————————

Joseph was a policeman in Miami, Florida at the time of his NDE. His experience began as a wonderful, peaceful one, but then changed to a Type III Less-Than-Positive Near-Death Experience. Joseph's story may sound familiar to you because he was featured on a CBS *48 Hours* show when they came to film our South Florida IANDS meeting. He had made a DUI arrest on highway I-95. While walking around to the trunk of his police car, he was shot at (but not injured) by a passenger in a car on the opposite side of the highway, then was actually hit by another vehicle. The driver of that vehicle hadn't seen either the police car or the DUI's car stopped on the shoulder of the highway. Joseph described his experience this way:

> All of a sudden I thought I was dreaming! It was like when you're a kid in a pool, going around in circles making fun flips. It was great! But I woke up inside the fire rescue truck and then I went out again and this is what happened.
>
> You'd have to picture a Western town converted into a Roman town. Everything was gray and black. There was a figure in front of me in a black hooded robe with long sleeves. He was around 5'7" tall. I was leaning, trying to see his face, but I couldn't. Behind him was a fountain that wasn't working, and to the left of me was a porch with Roman columns. To the right was a body shaking real, real hard. The figure in the hood was pointing down. There were people screaming. I felt cold. Across this little porch was another figure wrapped in, like, strips of canvas like a mummy, shaking, leaning against the wall. The screaming was horrible and I couldn't ell if it was coming from that thing or from all over the place. Then I panicked and tried to step over the figure the hooded guy was pointing at and, BOOM, I came to in ICU.

My girlfriend was in front of me when I came out of it in ICU. I wrote down on a pad what had happened and asked her to marry me. No pun intended, but that scared the hell out of me. I'm not saying that I believe in this, but I am saying that it definitely did happen. I did tell a priest what happened and he said religiously I was in a place that not too many people go to. I spoke to a scientist and he said that when the cortex of the brain is severely injured, like from losing 75 percent of my blood supply, it flashes memories of the brain and that it's really nothing. My arm was gone and had to be reattached. That's why I lost so much blood.

Joseph describes himself as a very skeptical person, saying that if a burning bush was in front of him, he would sit down and see what was causing the fire. He said:

I was brought up Catholic, but when I was in the Marines, before going into training to become a police officer, that went out the window. It's just the way it is. When I became a police officer I saw a lot of things that I didn't like and I didn't think there was a God. Before the accident I had three rental properties, and was buying more. I had my health, was in extremely good shape, and had a lot of money because I was also working, protecting the Sheik of Saudi Arabia when he was in Miami. I had been hungry for money. Now it doesn't matter. I guess I was a tough little kid arresting people. If you deserved to go to jail, then you went to jail. If you violated the law, that was it! So before I was a machine. Unfortunately, there's a lot of machines out there. Now, I'm a person.

What was the bottom line? Joseph saw what he needed to see and felt what he needed to feel in terms that were unique to his way of viewing the world. As a policeman, he was used to being in total control. In the LTP experience, it was the hooded figure who was in control. Interesting, too, was his description of the scene as a Western town converted into a Roman town, and that he even estimated the exact height of the hooded figure as he was trained to do. He said:

"When I was a kid we played cowboys and Indians and we'd kill the Indians. My ancestors were Spaniards and what they did to the Indians was inhumane. Believe it or not, I've asked for forgiveness. Since the accident, I'm for the Indians!"

Joseph, admittedly, did not have true respect for or value life prior to his experience. That has changed now. He said:

> I was arrogant and very tough. Now, life is everything. Everything deserves to live. Everything, even the big bug you go to squish. You cannot make a judgment about what does and doesn't die. A roach crawled up my leg when I was taking an exam last week. I just brushed it off. This is a roach, for God's sake, and yet I was hoping no one would step on it. There's nothing that should be killed. Humanity has a lot more to learn. There's just too much greed and too many people that are power-hungry out there.

Joseph does not have full use of his arm, so he can no longer work as a policeman. He is beginning law school, and plans to work as an advocate for the victims of crime. He did marry his girlfriend, has two wonderful children, and is enjoying being a loving, giving father.

There is a very interesting followup to Joseph's story. At one of the South Florida IANDS meetings, he met Charles Nunn, a metaphysical teacher and spiritual healer who was visiting from Virginia. (Charles' story is related in chapter eight.) Until that meeting Joseph had continued to be very distressed about his LTP experience, particularly with reference to why he had such a frightening episode. He received tremendous peace and solace from Charles Nunn's counsel and wisdom. Charles said at that meeting:

> We're discussing the condition of a person's mind, or their mindset or belief system, when they actually pass over. Joseph had asked why he had a "bad" experience and why I had a "good" experience. As I see it, the state of your mind at the time that you pass over makes the difference in what you actually experience on the other side.

Joseph was a police officer accustomed to risk. There's a certain amount of adrenaline rush when you stop to arrest somebody. In his job he was always at risk. He had arrested two DUIs that day, then [someone in] a carload of people from the other side of the highway fired at him. It was the day of the Rodney King verdict in Los Angeles. Joseph was shot at because those people were really angry at police officers because those in California were found "not guilty." So Joseph's adrenaline was already pumping, causing that fight-or-flight mechanism. He was in a defensive mode, knowing he was at risk and in danger. Therefore, when he passed over, the scenes that he would expect and the scenes he did, in fact, see, would be of a frightening nature.

The black-hooded figure apparently represented the grim reaper or the angel of death. He never saw his face, but saw the black hood on the down-turned head. Joseph kept trying to see his face. Had he seen it, then he would not have returned to life at this particular time. The dimension he was in appeared to be a very low part of the astral realm, where there is fear and darkness and despair. He saw the other beings there wrapped in white canvas, shaking uncontrollably. So he was shown that those people were fearful. That represented hell. I, personally, do not see hell as a place, but as a state of being. In that particular situation Joseph went over in fear, connected with violence, and so that is exactly what he experienced. When he stepped over one of those shaking beings he made a choice. It wasn't a mental choice, but an energetic response, to remove himself from that realm. When he did, he suddenly found himself back in the ICU.

I must say that Charles' comments spoke truth to my soul, as they did to Joseph's. It reinforced my belief that a "less than loving" (including a violent or fearful) mindset *immediately prior* to an NDE may certainly be instrumental in producing an LTP near-death experience. Coming from a place of love, rather than a place of fear and/or violence, may make the difference between a blissful NDE and an LTP.

It appears that disavowing the reality or possibility of the existence of a Higher Power may contribute to the "why" of a Less-Than-Positive Experience; 19.4 percent of my LTP study group labeled themselves as atheist or agnostic prior to their experience. If one also disrespects life, then that just compounds the problem.

Such was the case with Joel, who is now seventy-five years old, but was fifty-eight years old at the time of his first Near-Death Experience. Joel was raised in a Jewish home. After World War II, he became a pharmacist. He became a diabetic when he was in his forties and later developed many of the common complications of the disease. He stated:

> The first experience was when I was in the hospital with gangrene. They were marking the progression up my leg. The pain was horrendous. They decided to amputate the next day. I kept screaming: "I want to die. Hell with the leg!" During the surgery this is what happened. Out comes this ladder, right out of the heavens, like Jacob's ladder. And here's this angel, male, in a mist, dressed in a grayish-tan gauze overlay. The angel told me I have no right to want to die. He said that when God is ready, that's when I'll die. I tried to climb that ladder, but the angel had strong arms. I kept trying to get up there, and he slapped me, told me that only the Lord will decide and that I should stop complaining. Then he disappeared.
>
> I was out of the hospital for two weeks, didn't feel right, went to the ER and had to be readmitted with congestive heart failure. I developed bad pain in my side while I was there, had a workup and ended up with a colostomy because it was cancer. What the hell! Why not? That's when I had the second experience.
>
> Would you believe, here came the devil! There was a band of people, all dressed in black, all wearing shrouds with hoods, about eight of them and a leader. I said: "Oh, shit!" They all had candles. The leader had slanted eyes and I

thought maybe the Japs were after me. I was in the Pacific theater in World War II, so I know what Japs look like, but this was a tall son of a bitch! Nobody spoke. They just nodded and pranced around with the candles. If I'd had a gun I would've shot them.

They were out to kill me. That I believe. They didn't want me to live, maybe because I derided them. I don't believe in hocus pocus. It was the candles that threw me off, and the fact that I saw these slant eyes. I thought they were all Japs, but really knew they weren't. But they were people I didn't like. They wanted to do me harm and I was already in enough pain. I didn't want any more. I didn't need this bullshit! And then the surgery was over. It was awful surgery.

I was in there for five weeks. Toward the end of the hospitalization, BINGO, I was visited again, but this time it was just a voice. A male voice called my name.

It told me, in essence, to mind my p's and q's, not to get excited, and that I'm being tested. I asked: "For what?" I was admonished not to question, to take my medicine and if I don't like it to keep quiet. It also suggested that I do a little praying, and I'm "son-of-a-bitching" all over the place. I said: "Praying don't help me." The pain was unbelievable, because they had to clean and pack my open wound four times a day. I had said: "Just pull the pipes and let me go." The voice said: "You don't decide, He'll decide." Then, here comes this fella down the ladder again right out of the heavens, right out of the clouds. I said: "This time are you going to take me up the ladder?" The answer was: "No." In the meantime, back at the ranch, the surgeon was telling my family that there was no hope for me. My heart had stopped a couple of times, but here I am!

Afterwards, one of the rabbis came up to the room to see me. I told him that I wasn't interested in rabbis. I told him about the meeting with the Man from upstairs and I said to him that I don't want to live anymore. That rabbi took off his yarmulke and started to curse me. I have never heard anyone who could curse as well as I can. He asked me who the hell I thought I was. I told him to mind his own business and that he can go to hell and take his religion with him. I told him to get the hell away from me. He said: "Only God decides who lives and dies." I said: "I don't believe in God." He said that if I didn't believe in God, then I wouldn't see angels. I got so angry that I put the side rails down, got out of bed and fell, so they had to stitch me up and tie me down. I told him that I want to get the hell out of this life, no matter where I go, down below or wherever. And it must be something that all these rabbis learned way back, because he also said again: "God decides who lives and who dies." I told him: "During the war I didn't believe in God, and when they say there are no atheists in foxholes that's bullshit. When these priests come in and cross themselves, that's bullshit also. So don't come in here and start preaching."

The "why" of Joel's LTP was twofold. First, he kept wishing himself dead, and second, he said repeatedly that he didn't believe in God, even using the word "atheist." The LTP "suggested" to him that there is, in fact, a Higher Power, and that only that Higher Power has the authority to decide when one's life is over. The symbolism, Joel thinking that the group of shrouded figures with candles were led by a "Jap," goes back to his awful experience of being held captive by Japanese in WWII and the horrors that he endured there. Joel is a very visual person. Has he changed as a result of what happened? Yes, he has. He now goes to temple often, and does feel that there is a Higher Power.

Reggi had three Near-Death Experiences, two of which were Less-Than-Positives. Her childhood was very traumatic, in large part because she was molested by her father. She, as do many children in the same situation, used astral projection (going out of body) to escape the trauma. Reggi admits that she had "no respect for life" and also labeled herself an atheist prior to the NDEs. I shall present her two LTPs and then her very profound light experience. She said:

I guess between nine and ten I didn't really care if I lived or died. I tried not to breathe so I'd die, but God wouldn't let me. After that, let's face it Doc, I wasn't living the life I should have been living. I kind of went away from God. I didn't believe, and I was angry. I was actually an atheist. I believed in nothing.

I tried to OD one time to commit suicide, because my children and ex-husband were making it very difficult for me. I'd taken a bunch of Tuinals. I saw the devil. The floor opened up and he came out of it. He looked at me with these fiery eyes. He was wearing a ring with a goat's head on it. I looked at him and I said: "You're not getting me. You go back to hell!"

A few years after that I had survived a ninety-foot fall doing construction. I hit concrete and sand, face down, causing some brain damage. Then in the hospital they gave me the wrong medication, which I was allergic to, and my heart went berserk. I was in coma. Suddenly I was in like a Roman orgy, satanic type. I saw the devil. He communicated with me and raped me. I saw his face and heard his voice. I saw evil all around me, but all of a sudden I felt this pulling of my body. Way up high, I saw a tunnel of light. I went through the tunnel and heard voices which I recognized, because they were people I knew that had passed on. They all said: "Go back." I heard this three times. And I saw this black angel of death. He was a hooded man in a black robe. I couldn't see his face. He was reaching for my hand and just as I was going to take it he turned around, pointed at me and said: "Go back. It is not your time."

Reggi's last NDE was secondary to liver failure as a result of a post-hepatitis cirrhosis. She stated:

I felt as though something was pulling me from my body. You know where you get that gut feeling? Well, it was detachment from there. It was almost like you took a plunger and went "sloop." It was almost like your body was pulling down and your soul was pulling up, like you were taking taffy and pulling. I went through this tunnel of light. I heard voices there that I figured were my grandparents. When I got to the other end I actually saw Christ! He was smiling and standing with His arms open like He was going to hug me. I went to Him and He said: "You have to go back. You have premonitions. It is not your time yet. Go back."

I asked Reggi to describe Christ.

I was raised in Catholicism, but I don't think that had any bearing on anything. He was in a white robe, and there was kind of a blue aura around him, and gold around his head. He had a beard. He had the most beautiful blue eyes, almost like a husky blue, like a Siberian husky, crystal blue. He looked about thirty-six, like He looked on the cross. He wasn't very tall, about 5'9" or 5'10" at the most. His arms were stretched out as if to hug me. He wasn't wearing sandals. He was just in a white robe, like if you just took a sheet and put it over your body, with some sort of a gold cord around his waist. His skin was so white it was like a dove. Flawless skin, so clean and so heavenly, just like a fluorescent bulb. He had brown shoulder-length hair with, like, streaks of gold in it. He telepathically spoke. He communicated with a look. I knew what He was saying without Him opening His mouth. His hands still carried the marks of the cross. He still had the puncture marks, and there was light going through them, laser light. And when I looked down I noticed He had the marks of the nails on His feet.

There was a white mist, and the light was so bright it was almost like the sun and the fury. There is such a peace and such a calm, and the love is just an outpouring. There is so much love coming from every direction. Everything was in technicolor. It was the most beautiful place I've ever seen. There was grass and flowers with every fragrance, like fine perfumes.

I saw spirits that were kind of transparent. There was no real form, but just an outline. You could almost see a cellophane person. They had no substance, but you could see a face and everything. You could tell who they were, but you could look through them. They were all in white robes and they all looked like angels, no wings, but angels. I saw people I knew and people I didn't know. It was just an outpouring of love like a chain, everyone was holding hands. It was like everybody just came there to see you in.

I had the most elated love feeling I've ever had. It surpasses orgasm. It surpasses everything you could possibly think of. It is the highest feeling that you can feel. It's euphoric, very euphoric. There's just no pain after death. It's so peaceful that you don't want to come back. I screamed and cried when I came back into my body.

One can easily tell by how Reggi described her three NDE events that her model of the world is primarily visual. I present her experiences, including the profoundly luminous one, in such detail because I feel it is an excellent example of proving that what one needs is exactly what one gets. I feel that she needed to see Christ and feel His forgiveness and needed confirmation that He existed. She did not need to have a life review because she was acutely aware of her previous indiscretions with drugs, her suicide attempt, and her admitted atheism. The significant life-altering changes have been ongoing. In her words:

I've changed my values. I did a 360. I hate no one. I love everyone. Now I'm a caring, giving person. Money means nothing to me. I got $80,000 and spent $40,000 helping my kids and people I know. Material things don't matter any more. People liking you and you loving them is the most important thing. I have forgiven my father.

I think more cautiously and try to not take chances. You come back more level-headed than when you left. Your right and wrong is really straightened out when you come back. You come back as a do-gooder. You come back with so much love, it's like a hand-basket. You absolutely have no negative. Everything is positive. The world is your family. Any color becomes your family. You take strangers in. You take animals in. You're outpouring love everywhere. The nurturing got stronger. You come back with a sense of feeling strong. You know things nobody knows. The calm is incredible. It's like the eye of the storm. You have such peace within, yet you fear nothing and no one. It is incredible! It's constant euphoria. I don't need drugs to stay high. I think we beam up like a laser. I think that's how He pulls us through. And I think God's light is like a laser light.

You asked me if I felt any judgment. No. I think hell is here on earth. You see, we are not judged by the bad we do, we are judged by the good. If you keep doing bad then your soul keeps coming back to earth. And if you never do it right then we just stay here forever. But we are here to learn. It's a learning process, and once we learn we go forward. I feel you reach heaven when you reach perfection.

Reggi now has her own ministry and does spiritual counseling.

———————

Dr. Francis Ceravolo, a family practitioner in Fort Lauderdale, told me this story about a patient who was a professed atheist:

I was present when one of my patients coded five times in the ER. He is an Italian man whom I've known for many years. He's a very calm, nice gentleman, just as nice as you would ever want to meet. He admitted to me that he didn't believe in God. He told me after he was revived: "I saw fire and I saw little creatures, about four-and-a-half, max five feet tall, all around me. They were bad-looking, terrible creatures. I saw them every time I died. I knew every time I died." He believes in God now, because he knows he survived only because God allowed him to.

———————

Several people who had LTP experiences had in common a feeling of ambivalence about experimenting with hypnotherapy and past life regression, and searching out other realities. Stephanie, fifty-three, had her experience at age thirty. She was hospitalized with a 105-degree temperature, secondary to a severe bacterial infection that was going through her bloodstream. She stated:

> **My whole body lifted straight up, just floated out, but I think there was something connecting me, like a tow rope, although I couldn't see it. First I went into darkness and then into a very long tunnel and then into the most beautiful valley that you have ever seen in your life. There was beautiful green, and flowers, and the bluest sky. I was thrilled to be there. Way off in the distance I saw a beautiful woman coming toward me. She was in a flowing robe. I was going toward her. The closer she got to me, her features started to change. Her face became like a bear, then another animal, then another, then at the end her face turned into this, like, boar's face with tusks and slobber, and I started to freak out. Then I was pulled back into my body. It was like hitting the water when you dive into a swimming pool.**

Stephanie is a very visual person, dresses in vivid colors, and decorates in bright colors. She is now owner of a company and uses her own resources to help underprivileged children. She feels she had the experience as a warning that what she was "delving into was evil." She feels that she *needed* to have that experience. She was raised in the Baptist faith. She said:

> **If you were good, you went to heaven. If you were bad, you went to hell. It was the old-time Baptist damnation: hell fire and brimstone. I had fear of God as a child. They ruled through fear. But now I believe that God is not a God of damnation. I know now that the Bible was written by humans and in a manner to control, especially the part about hell. Before the experience I had started going to meetings of the Inner Peace movement. I got to where I could see auras and**

did mild laying on of hands. And I could blurt out things that would happen. I went through many sessions on hypnosis. I spoke six different languages under hypnosis, although I never studied more than English. And I went through regression therapy to a past life in Egypt. I came to feel all of that was wrong for me, and that's probably why I had that scary experience, so I would stop messing with things that I shouldn't be messing with.

Jack Cuthrell, friend and author of *Letters of the Soul . . . From the Silence of the Mind* (Spiritual Quest, 1995), told me about the following experience that an acquaintance had. The gentleman, who we shall call Xaviar, was driving alone through the Badlands in the West, where there were long stretches of open road. He developed severe chest pain (which was a heart attack), jammed on the brakes, and got out. He looked back and saw his body, then proceeded to walk into the Badlands. It seemed that the winding path was just for him. On both sides of the path, at irregular intervals, were large holes from which appeared demons and semireptilian humans reaching out trying to grab him. He felt apprehensive but not surprised. After he successfully made it through that ordeal, the LTP changed to a usual joyful one, where he encountered deceased relatives.

Significant in Xaviar's life is the fact that he was a concentration camp survivor in Germany, in WWII. He regarded the Near-Death Experience basically as a replay of his life. He felt that the demons represented the Nazis. He told Jack: "If you could make yourself keep going and survive the camps then you can survive anything." His LTP experience, therefore, was actually a reward. It confirmed to him that his loved ones who had not survived "the ovens" are fine and that they will eventually all be together again.

LTP experiences may occur to those expecting to be judged. Those experiencers were often raised in deeply religious families and were taught to expect hell fire and brimstone if they were "deserving of it." One of the treasures of the NDE and most LTPs is that the only judgment that occurred was by the person judging himself. Only a few subjects felt that they were judged by another being. The very distressing part of the LTP, which may contain that life review, sometimes converts to a wonderful spiritual experience. The particular need of the soul is fulfilled. Not only may the soul become healed, but often the body as well. The following account is representative.

Rudolph is a delightful gentleman who had his NDE in 1996 at fifty-three years of age. He grew up in a straight-laced, very strict Irish Catholic family, the youngest of nine children. He said that he hated growing up, always felt that he wanted to be somewhere else, and felt he could never accomplish things fast enough. He divorced from his wife and, at that point, had to deal with his homosexuality. He had been the first lay principal of a Catholic school, so he was put on a pedestal and had a tremendous struggle in dealing with the Catholicism issue once he came out of the closet with the homosexuality. He stated:

> I have AIDS, which was diagnosed in 1989. I got liver toxicity from the protease inhibitors, turned completely yellow, and had to be admitted to the hospital. I had twenty blood transfusions because my blood didn't clot, then I was able to have my gallbladder surgery. Then, suddenly, my liver and kidneys both crashed. The doctors admitted they didn't know what to do for me. I refused dialysis. I don't know why, but I knew I wouldn't die.
>
> I was in the hospital bed, in kidney and liver failure, and suddenly there was this harsh sound like the roof was being moved. Then, suddenly, I was surrounded by smoke, then the flames started and I was engulfed in the flames. I could hear myself screaming and screaming. Then, above me, I saw rats running around and dirt flying everywhere. It was the scariest

thing! It was so real! Then, as quickly, that was over and I was immediately transported to this other very peaceful, real bright place and there was this angel there. She was wearing traditional angel clothes, the white gown, and wings. She was fairly young, in the thirty range, with brown, medium-length hair. I felt love from her. I felt peaceful. She said: "We want you to go back." I asked her why I had to go back. I said: "Tell me what my purpose is. What is my reason for living?" She said it was because I was a teacher. I told her that I wasn't anymore and she said: "Even though you are no longer a formal teacher at the university, everyone you touch you teach and you are going to be touching a lot of people. That's your purpose. Go back and teach and love people and just be yourself."

Then I was in yet another place again, very peaceful. I'd had a lover for seven years who died of AIDS in 1989. When he died he looked very ill, very emaciated. But there he was and he was an angel! He had very long blond hair. He always called me "Rudie." He said: "Rudie, you can't stay. You're not finished. You have too much to do there." He told me: "You're on earth for a very short time. Where you are going afterward you will be going forever, so enjoy what you can while you are on earth." We actually talked about friends, how they're doing, and how I was coping. He told me to enjoy my grandson and let him get to know me. Now, he had been dead for seven years when my grandson was born. I told him: "I don't think I have the energy to go back." And I remember that at that point I clutched my chest, not with pain, but it was this burst of energy in my chest, my heart, and then I was back in the hospital bed.

The specialist said to me: "You shouldn't be alive. There is nothing the doctors did for you. We did absolutely nothing. I don't know what you believe in, but you should believe in a Higher Power." My kidneys functioned at 100 percent. The kidney failure was gone and my liver started to get steadily better.

There are many significant life-altering changes post-NDE, both physical and spiritual. Rudie came back essentially healed of his renal failure from the NDE. Even more significant to him is that he no longer fears death, and he has come to terms with his HIV. He said about the AIDS:

> I call it my tragic gift. It's tragic because of all the devastation it's caused and all the lives that have been lost. But it's a gift, because I've really grown to know who I am and have been allowed to meet so many wonderful people. It's my best friend and my worst friend. I hate it and I love it. You never get rid of it. It's always with you.

Rudie has also now totally come to terms with the homosexuality issue. He said:

> What I'm doing now is probably one of the most productive times in my life. I have an excellent grasp of people. I'm working on a lot of boards. I'm working to eliminate homophobia. We are normal people. We're not the stereotypical people that they think we are. I got the President's award for vision and leadership of the association I started. My goal is to see corporations accept openly gay and lesbian employees and include not only sexual orientation in their policies but partner benefits and everything else. We want equal rights!

It was most important and significant that in the experience he felt no judgment whatsoever. Remember, his deceased lover, after bodily death, became an angel! He saw him with a healthy, strong etheric body. His friend knew of the new grandson who had been conceived and born after his death. That further confirmed to Rudie that the experience was real, and confirmed to him that he is being watched over.

Rudie was told that he was to touch people through teaching. He said:

> I've been speaking at the university about living with AIDS. When you work with AIDS patients you have to help them find meaning, because if you don't then they are going to die.

You find meaning in your life and you find a purpose and you find value. I think that summarizes why we're here. But each of us has to find that out for ourselves.

Rudie considers himself primarily a kinesthetic, or feeling, type person. In the experiences, it was the feelings that were most significant for him, more than what he saw or heard. He did, indeed, feel, hear, and see what he needed to in order to bring about changes in his attitudes toward his disease, lifestyle, and fear of death. He found new meaning and purpose to his life and is sharing it with others. His renal and liver disease were physically healed and his soul received a healing as well. The LTP followed by the transcendental light experience was truly a blessing.

Sadira is another very kinesthetic person. She is a nurse and has cared for cancer patients for many years. She had her Type III Less-Than-Positive Near-Death Experience as a result of an overdose. In her words:

I didn't care if I woke up or not. I didn't know why I was so depressed, but it was like I was saying: "God, I'm putting it in your hands." I don't know if I stopped breathing, but I was unconscious.

What I saw was the most hideous, horrible thing! This was no nightmare! If you saw the movie *Ghost*, it was like where those horrible black things came out and were grabbing you. There were people screaming. It was unearthly voices, not earthly. It was horrible!

These things were all over me and they were screaming. I think I was naked there, because I remember feeling very ashamed. Everything was dark. I couldn't tell where the screaming was coming from. Then I actually saw these things, like horrible human beings, like anorexics. Their teeth were all ugly and twisted. The eyes were bulging. They were bald, no hair, and weren't wearing anything. They were naked!

There must have been at least fifty, everywhere, all around me. They were grabbing at my arms and my hair, and were screaming, pitiful screams, but not saying words. It was the type of moaning and screaming that you hear in a cancer ward, God forbid.

Then I saw them in my room, and I saw me in my room. Then I must have gone to a different plane, because then I could actually feel their breath next to me. They were wet, like sweaty, and they smelled so foul, like a rotting thing, like death. I've smelled dead rats which didn't smell as bad as this. Everything was just so vivid!

I felt judged. I felt that was my punishment. Those beings were there to punish me, but they didn't physically hurt me because I don't recall feeling pain. I just remember the pure terror! Then, slowly, the screaming started to get further away. It's like they were moving into another room to torture someone else.

Naturally, as Catholics, we're taught that we aren't to take our own lives, because that means you've lost faith in God. I can tell you this: there is no way I will ever think of attempting suicide ever again, or ever take that attitude. It was just so horrific! I went to hell! I went to hell! And I don't remember being redeemed! I don't remember any good part of it. I don't remember calling out for God and God rescuing me. I just remember waking up. We were taught that hell was a non-consuming fire, that it burns and hurts but doesn't actually burn the tissue. Personally, I never believed in hell. I believed that hell was not being able to see God. But after this, I believe in hell.

When I woke up I felt absolutely terrified, yet with a renewed hope. Suicide can never be the answer. This is not an option. God does not want this. I believe in God very strongly. He will not excuse this. I saw hell!

I do a lot more for myself now. I used to be very dependent on my family. This experience did just totally change my life. Now I'm glad it happened!

It is my feeling that what happened to Sadira was just exactly what was needed to show her that suicide is wrong. She agrees that she got just exactly what she needed. She knows, now, that she is responsible for all of her choices, and that every second of this lifetime counts. Now she takes full responsibility for all of those choices.

———————

Yolanda had a combination of the Type II and Type III LTP, then a life review, and then "a personal encounter with God," during which she became spiritually enlightened. This was secondary to the trauma of losing a baby. Her spiritual growth has been tremendous. She stated:

> I had the hell, the in-between, and the heaven experience. First I was in a dark, cool place. I felt beings around me, but didn't see them. At the end of the dark place was a light, a cold light, and I was being pushed toward it by these invisible presences. The closer I got the more evil it felt. Finally I got close enough to see, though this'll sound weird, but it looked like the gates of hell with millions of big demon eyes looking through it. It was very cold and I was terrified! I knew it was hell and I didn't want to go there. Then, somehow, I started going backwards the other way.
>
> I went into this gray void where it felt like there was absolutely nothing at all, like I was in outer space. I was floating, but didn't have control and was stuck, trapped, and scared to death. Then came this sound from deep down inside me calling out: "God, God." That's when I did like a life review thing. It like zipped on, but it was more concentrated at the end, so the last years came out real clear. I saw everything that I had ever done to that day, and that it was meaningless and useless and it had brought me to that place. I felt very weak and hopeless and useless.
>
> This is weird, but when I called out to God, a kind of light, like spiritual lightning, struck my head and went through me, and then something inside me exploded. When this happened

I felt like a crackling and tingling in my mind, in my brain, and I felt tingling through my whole body and every cell became energized and alive. It was traumatizing, but it was wonderful. And the light, just like you read about, was just all knowledge, all life, all beauty, and all love. It was saying: "No, you're not THAT person, THIS is who you are. I love you, totally and unconditionally." I believed that was coming from God. There was some actual voice messages and the rest was in my mind, like a knowing. I was told: "You're making this all too complicated" and that "'here is nothing on earth that matters except learning to love and receive love." That's what it's all about. God is everything. Energy is everything.

After this the whole world was different. Everything was alive and pulsating with this beautiful energy, and I was awe-struck. Now I really see the beauty in people, but I can also see that some people are blind to their own so they don't let it come out. I grew up in another country where there was a lot of religion, but a lot of killing, too. Because of that, I became agnostic, not so much about God, but about my Christian religion. The God I met in the experience was totally different from the God I had learned about.

Yolanda describes herself as a visual and auditory person. This experience spoke to her directly in terms that she needed. She feels now that "even what one would consider a bad experience can be turned into something good." She said that what she most needed before the experience was to feel loved, and that is what she brought away with her. She learned that she had received mixed and erroneous messages in her upbringing. It awakened her spirituality. She has now come to realize that everything is connected.

There is a unity and every tiny little thing has purpose and definition and meaning. It all has to do with spiritual insight. You can look in the Yellow Pages and find spirituality if your eyes are open, and you can read the Bible and walk straight to hell if they're closed!

I realized after I came through that experience that I'd always felt that I'd been doomed to be either the shadow or the saint, but there's a special place in between that is the human being. That part I had totally denied. I realized during this that being human is beautiful. Being a human being, not having to be an animal, not having to be God, but being in that place in between is beautiful.

The Place Between Heaven and Hell

At least a couple of subjects described viewing a "way station to hell" on the way to a luminous Near-Death Experience. Chad, an architect, had his NDE when he slipped into a diabetic coma secondary to pneumonia. His description:

> There was a swirling, boiling hum and I was in a sheer cloud bank. And there was a limit. I saw people and everything, like boiling in and out of it, like an arm would come out and boil back in and then a leg. I remember a horse. It was seething. People and animals and birds were trying to get through, but they were sucked back in. I think it was probably a way station to hell. I think it was here. It was earth. It's everything that's going on here. I think we're in hell here, but we can certainly make it worse.

Tim attends nearly every one of our South Florida IANDS meetings. He has been my medical patient for many years. His occupation was selling insurance until in his mid-forties when he became disabled with cirrhosis, secondary to infectious hepatitis that he contracted when in school. During the time he was undergoing a liver transplant he had a Near-Death Experience. He also saw people "in a swirl." He explains:

> First I was standing like on a dark, black, crunchy rock, like the terrain of the moon would be, or like black cinder like a volcano. As I walked, I crunched. I never left that. I could see millions of people, like in a swirl, but you couldn't identify

them. They were shrouded and dark, but I knew my mother, deceased, was among them. I knew she was pleased that somehow my life had taken a turn for the better now.

It was misty. I saw some angels floating by and there was incredibly beautiful music, perfect music. It was angelic music. I knew I was sinking and I didn't have the strength to come back. First, what terrors I went through! It was like being in an aquarium, being chased by fish that were all trying to get you or bite you. There's no place to go. You can't go up or down or hide. The pain is intense and you're spending every ounce of energy that you have trying to escape from these horrible things. It's kind of a suspended period. That's when you go through the giving up process, but I fought and fought and fought.

Then all of a sudden there was Calvin! (Calvin is his closest living friend.) His heritage is American Indian. He believes in both Christianity and the Great Spirit. Then, to my right, there appeared to be three men with white hair and white garments, almost biblical. They were judges. It appeared like I was being judged. I was just standing there. My native American friend, who was standing like on a ridge, walked by and shouted extremely loudly to these judges: "You can't take him. I'm taking him back." Then the whole thing was over. It was so real, I couldn't get it out of my mind! When I called Calvin to tell him what had happened, he told me that at the exact same time he had an identical dream.

I learned a lot from this. What matters most in life, ironically, isn't the material things, but it's the loyalty and the sharing that most people pretend to have but don't really. Their life is going by in a twirl, and they're living an empty life. My mother did that for years after she divorced my father. It was a sad thing and a real waste.

Tim never felt that his mother approved of his lifestyle. He was able to get the approval he needed from her in the experience. He felt that he came away with exactly what he needed: understanding from his mother, and loyalty from his friend. He loves music, so that was an important aspect for him. Interestingly, he loves cats and hates fish—that may be why the aquarium was present.

LTP Near-Death Experiences of Children

There can be no question that negative programming during childhood can be instrumental in causing a Less-Than-Positive Near-Death Experience should a serious situation (such as an illness) arise. Connie Sterling, a friend, said about her childhood: "I grew up having been told that hell is down at the center of the earth. I was told you would descend down stairs, like to a very dark cave where there are fires burning. I was taught to picture the devil as a hairy male with horns and a tail and a pitchfork." My hope is that all parents, all future parents, and all teachers will take heed to this warning. When one programs a sweet young soul with the threat of hell fire and brimstone, then that is what that sweet soul may project to the cosmos and that is what will be experienced in a near-death, death, or other traumatic situation. Please, please, please, do not do this to our children!!!

Kay has been a wonderful supporter of our South Florida IANDS support and study group since its beginning in October, 1996. It has positively transformed her life to know that she is not alone in her experience, and to understand why it happened. She said of her experience:

> I had what you would call a hellish experience when I was three years old. I had died prior to that with pneumonia. The doctor had put me on heavy sulfa drugs and I stopped breathing. . . . I remember it was sort of like a half dream. I saw what I think I knew to be a hell. It was like a very deep, dark pit or cave, like maybe down under the earth. There were fires burning, and tall stairways coming down, chiseled out of the

earth. There were people coming down the stairway, from where I don't know. They seemed to be very miserable, unhappy people, moaning, in a lot of pain and agony. I know that I picked up on the things that I must have heard early in Church Sunday School, so that's why I thought it must've been hell. I do remember looking around for the boogie man or the devil, the guy with a tail and pitchfork, but I never did see that being. I never did see any evil being, but in a child's mind it was a definite feeling of evil and misery, and just a horrible place to be. It happened when I was too young to know good from evil. I'm so grateful to hear in these meetings that I'm not the only one to have had such an experience at a young age!

Chris has also been one of South Florida IANDS greatest supporters. Immediately after he heard Kay's account, he stated:

That's really fascinating! When I was a child I had a lot of fevers. I remember being in that place five or six times. There was this huge pit with walls that went straight up. I didn't see any people or make any connection with the devil, but there were these huge monsters which were like probably the biggest brown bears on the planet. At every path to get out was one of these huge bears. I was panicked and scared looking for a way out, but there was none. I don't remember any heat, but I do remember a bright red canyon, a bright red wall, and the big huge bears hollering and screaming. It scared me so bad that I actually soaked the bed with sweat! So when I was sick, I was afraid to go to sleep!

Here is one more example. Sandra had an illness with a very high fever as a child. She stated:

I was three or four and we lived up north at the time. I was very sick. I had this dream. Even after all these years later it is still vivid. I was in this very dark place, and all of a sudden there were a whole bunch of faces. They were closing in on me, with this demonic laugh. They had a strand of pearls. They told me to take the pearls, but said that one would explode. I took off each pearl, one by one. One did explode into this thick glitter with a whole bunch of glittery dust that was really soft. Then I looked up and again all these people were closing in on me with that same demonic laugh. It was a horrible feeling. That place was just dark, with no bottom and no end.

Years later Sandra was truly blessed to have a profoundly blissful NDE that included an encounter with Christ. It was during a cardiac arrest while undergoing a hysterectomy. She has had multiple spiritually transforming events since.

Now that we have a good grasp of the Type III LTP experience, we will discuss the Type IV in the next chapter.

SIX

Type IV LTP:
The Frightening
Life Review

$\mathcal{I}$n addition to the three types of distressing Near-Death Experiences described by Greyson and Bush, I suggest that there is also a fourth type. Several members of my study group were frightened specifically by the life review that they endured. Some perceived that they were being judged by a Higher Power, which sometimes took the form of a tribunal. The data shows that 33.3 percent of Type I, 30 percent of Type II, and 20 percent of the Type III experiencers had a life review, also, as part of their experience.

My life is a trial and I am guilty.

—C. W. Metcalf

Some Examples of the Type IV LTP Experience

Morris called in to a radio program in South Florida where I was a guest of Dr. Craig Anderson and Kari Sommerfield, and I subsequently interviewed him. He grew up as a

Zion Baptist and had his experience in 1993 when he was in his twenties. His occurrence was the result of severe depression. (We are reminded that identical experiences can occur without clinical death.) He said:

> I was at a point in my life where everything was just coming apart. Everything just went wrong. I wasn't happy with life. My company was closing, a girl I loved with all my heart just wouldn't settle down, and that took a toll on me. I was very upset with a situation that occurred when I was a young child, which was my father's death. I was told that he had put a gun in his mouth and blew his brains out. So everything came crashing down in my life and I moved to Atlanta, as if there could be a geographic cure.
>
> That night, with my eyes closed, I said to God: "I'm really hurtin' right now and I don't know if I can make it. Take the good deeds that I've done and help someone else, but take me home." That's when it started. I was suddenly seeing stars all around, and suddenly there was this incredible marble seat and God was sitting on it! He had the bearded face of a man of wisdom, with a long, flowing, white beard, very full with hair. Chills went down my body. I've come to learn what those chills mean. It shook me. My whole body was electric! The Man was very upset with me because I had lost my faith. He said: "You are NOT my son, but your purpose is to be alive and on the earth." He had helped me so many times.
>
> All of those occurrences were what flashed back. All those times in my life that I had gone right to the point of death, I saw. Death didn't happen, because in stepped a guardian angel. It was designed to wake me up. That life review was so startling it scares me to death! Everything came through as feelings, feelings of the memories from a mindset, because my eyes were focused on Him. There was no changing of the scenery. It was a feeling, and the feeling represented a picture. God judged me in that life review. He humbled me to my knees. Now there are no corridors I can hide in. He's pulled every place I could run to away. It took a few years for this to

click in. I'm so naive, that's why God has been cracking my skull for so long to wake me up.

When you ask me what I think was the bottom line to why it happened, I have to say this: I kind of went over the edge this time and I pushed real hard and the Big Man knocked me flat on my butt. But at the same time He said: "Listen to what I'm telling you. This is real!" I know my task for this lifetime is to see if I can get through these hardships, gain the knowledge, and grow. I had been turned into an aggressor from my family pattern and I've had to learn how to transcend that aggressor personality. But I'm a 100 percent believer in reincarnation. I've been here before and that's what's pulled me through many, many times. I realize when I leave here that I can't go until the Big Man orders me home, but I'm coming back unless I fulfill everything this time around. Guess you could say I've surfed the universe, and I know what's out there.

Morris is obviously a kinesthetic person. He described his experience more with reference to feelings than to the visual or auditory aspects. He did need to review this lifetime and the choices he had made, including his choices of behavior. He stated that perhaps the most significant thing he "came away with" was that he now knows the purpose for which he is here.

I've come to realize that my purpose is that I'm a forerunner for something. That may be a little conceited. There's a very big purpose in my life, there's a reason I listened to the radio and let you come through this big stone wall that I put up.

In over 300 interviews, the only time that an interviewee has felt judged by anyone but themselves was in a Less-Than-Positive Near-Death Experience. Usually it was when suicide was either contemplated or attempted. The feeling of being judged by the most highly respected being, or other beings on the astral plane, then caused the experiencer to judge him- or herself and instigate change.

———————

Sandra was raised in the Pentecostal religion and grew up "expecting to be judged." She had an NDE five years ago, brought on by trauma. It was, indeed, the life review which she experienced that turned the NDE into an LTP experience. She said that she found herself out of her body, and immediately was reliving her life.

> I went back to all kinds of situations that I had been in. I felt a lot of guilt, a lot of shame, and a lot of judgment. It was all self-judgment but I know now that it was all from previous programming. Actually, I felt like I was defending my life.

Sandra's life review was still so painful that she couldn't bring herself to describe the specifics. She has done a tremendous amount of reading and a tremendous amount of soul-searching since that time. She said:

> My perception is that we experience life through our conditioning and our programming. A child doesn't have a rational mind. He doesn't have an ego. Everything he is told goes in, creating a belief system. In my instance, I took on the beliefs of my family and my religion, but religions were originally created for control, and so I felt tremendous judgment. If you're brought up to believe in hell, then you may just experience it. I did experience it, but I know now that it was in my program. I was taught a fear-based philosophy, rather than focusing on the positives.

Sandra definitely felt that her experience was predictable, given her particular upbringing and beliefs. She, too, called it her "major wake-up call." She said: "Here was something that appeared to be negative and ended up being probably the most positive experience for me. It's nice that what I've learned from it may help someone else. That's what it's all about!" We do NOT have to accept our previous programming. We have that choice. Sandra proved that. The LTP gave her exactly what she needed and she has grown because of it.

Twenty-nine-year-old Anita was referred to me by her pulmonologist, Dr. George Azar. Her boyfriend found her without a heartbeat and respiration. Anita had overdosed. She was resuscitated by the emergency medical team, was taken to the hospital and remained in intensive care on a respirator for nearly two weeks.

The first thing I remember is feeling like I was being restrained, like I couldn't move, and there was no reason I couldn't move. I'm one of those people who can't stand to be tied up. Finally, I did get loose and I know this will sound strange, but there were people walking around in what I thought were white uniforms. I thought I was on the deck of a cruise ship. I was trying to find my way out. Finally, I was able to break free, like from the upper part of my body.

The room I was in first was small and white. There wasn't anything there but a bed and a chair. I looked at myself. I was in the bed and I looked like hell. I broke free, first from the upper part of my body, and then I was walking through the corridors. That's when I saw my grandfather.

My grandfather had died about a year before. I told him I wanted to leave and he wouldn't let me. He was in a grumpy mood, which was always how he was. He was very stubborn. He said: "What the hell are you thinking? You're not going anywhere. Go back to your room." I thought this was very strange. He was wearing like a white robe, which was not his usual dress, and he was wearing a gray-blue shirt underneath and nothing on his feet. He was standing in front of a door to a room that I wanted to get into, but he wouldn't let me. Where I was it was cold and dark. The room I couldn't get into I knew was warm and had sunlight and sky. I knew the beach was there.

There was a man standing with my grandfather. He looked like Jesus Christ, with long hair and a beard and mustache. He had on simple clothing and sandals on his feet. I didn't really confront Him at all, but I knew He was mad, though, because He was carrying the same expression as my grandfather, which was very disapproving. They were not going to let me past them. Basically, they were like Gestapo.

It was then that I saw everything that I ever did wrong. I was on trial. It was strange. I saw things that happened years and years ago that I couldn't even remember in my own consciousness. It was like they were judging. Any white lie or any little fib and stuff like that seemed to pop up. It was like anything mean that you ever did to somebody, whether you meant to hurt them or not, came up. You know, you may not consciously want to hurt somebody, but you do it anyway. It was like a big broad sweep where I saw all the bad things I ever did. Honestly, it felt like I was in hell already. I felt like I was being judged for absolutely every single thing I had ever done. As far as what's right or wrong, I had always been pretty clear on that, but I think everybody has the capability of telling little white lies. They're nothing that would seen to hurt anybody, but you hurt yourself in the long run.

After I saw all of that, my grandfather said I had to go back, and I knew I did if he said so. I remembered what his wrath could be like from when I was younger. I always trusted him, though. He was a good man even if he was grumpy. So I went back to my room. I felt alone in that room. I kept waiting, and it seemed like I waited forever. Then, finally, I felt restricted again, and there I was back in my body.

Now I know I'm here for a purpose. I still don't know what it is, but this gave me a kick in the butt to tell me I'd better find out what I'm supposed to be doing on this fine planet. I guess if I'm going to be honest now, I'd better tell you that I was trying to take the easy way out. I am a fighter and I don't give up easily, but I *was* trying to give up.

Anita admitted that she had been an atheist. It is understandable that in the experience she perceived that she saw Christ, who was judging her and giving her disapproving looks. Also, it is interesting that the very stern grandfather, whom she loved and respected, was also there. Her life review taught her that lying and hurting others is wrong. Anita describes herself as a kinesthetic person, so it was significant that she felt bound and restricted when in her body, and cold. In her view of the world, the corridors resembled decks on a ship rather than a tunnel, and the white robes reminded her of cruise personnel uniforms. We do interpret things according to our previous experience and knowledge on the earth plane. After she recuperated she made a total about-face, made amends to people she knew she had wronged, and even moved away from Florida, which she termed the "drug capital of the world."

———————

Ana Jo is a lovely lady whom I met when I lectured to the Academy of Religion and Psychical Research. In her Near-Death Experience she encountered a tribunal. She said:

> I found myself in a lovely wooded area with a pathway which I walked along. Suddenly, suspended from a sky, was a stairway. I stepped onto the stairway and kind of floated up to a room that was also suspended in the sky. It had walls. The door was just an open doorway. It seemed to be marble construction, of a creamy beige color. Along either side were tables set up. There were individuals behind, seated along the tables all the way down, but I could not discern their faces. They were in spirit. I walked to the far end, and there was a table like this one, where three people sat. And I found myself on trial before a tribunal, for either something I hadn't done or something I had done. I don't know what it was. I wept. I knew I was in trouble. Then the person in the middle of the three said: "Go, you have your instructions." I turned around and was walking out. A master teacher stepped out from one of the tables. I know I remembered him from somewhere. He was a spiritual teacher. He walked out with me to the doorway. As I was coming down the stairway, I knew I'd been given a second chance to correct whatever I'd done wrong.

Aristotle wrote something that seems to sum up this situation: "The unexamined life is not worth living." The life review can be a blessing if one has been kind and treated his fellow man as he would wish to be treated, or it can seem like a curse if he is shown Less-Than-Positive actions taken in the past.

In the life review, the individual experiences the ripple effect of their actions, good and bad. One may see the soft touch on someone's shoulder, a smile, and hear kind, heartwarming words spoken, but he is also shown the things that he or she made a commitment to but never followed through with, as well as the negativity of lies, gossiping, and so forth.

Studying these life reviews, and knowing that all of us will experience one when we are finally on the other side, has changed me for the better. In a deeply meditative state, I did my own very detailed life review a couple of years ago. I asked for strength, clarity, guidance, protection, and insight. I asked, and I certainly received. Events that I had totally forgotten about on a conscious level surfaced in 3D and technicolor, along with all the associated feelings. I also felt the ripple effect of my actions, words, and even my prayers, upon others. How many incidents comprise a life? How many moments? I re-experienced true joy and happiness, but also deep, overwhelming sadness and hurt. I felt pride as well as shame. It helped me understand myself and understand how I came to be who I am. It is true that we are the sum total of every single experience and every single second of our lifetime to this point in time. I'd like to share just a couple of those moments that turned out to be great learning experiences. The lessons are universal.

Thomas à Kempis said: "Man sees your actions. God sees your motives." Did you ever say something so awful that it has squeezed your heart every time you've thought about it, wishing you could take it back? When I was a little girl my violin teacher, Mr. Applebaum, came to the house every week for my lesson. My sweet,

Russian-born, cherublike grandmother would sit quietly nearby every afternoon as I practiced for my weekly lesson. She sat in her Lincoln rocker with her legs covered with a crocheted afghan. Our dog, Winkie, sat next to her with his head on her lap. Every so often she would smile and nod and "conduct" the imaginary orchestra as I played. One week I didn't practice. I don't know why. As I reviewed it and relived it at the same time, I reexperienced that awful self-imposed guilt.

When Mr. Applebaum rang the doorbell, I felt that rush of shame. I knew I'd be found out. I lashed out at my sweet little grandma. I said: "Go away. You embarrass me sitting there." She looked at me with the saddest eyes I've ever seen. They were welling up with tears, but she didn't say a word. She slowly and painfully got up on her creaky arthritic knees and went into the other room. The dog followed. That violin lesson lasted a good three hours, since we had to do a whole week of practicing before the new lesson. My heart wasn't in it and my violin knew. You see, a violin won't sing for someone who has been hateful.

My grandmother never told my father what I had said. She never brought it up. I never brought it up. I never said I was sorry and that I loved her dearly. I don't think I've said many hateful things in my life since. The hurt that you cause someone else can actually stay with you like a gray, suffocating cloud. My lesson? If we do "misspeak," then just as soon as we can, we need to say we're sorry, even if it is years later. Or, if we haven't said something that we should have said, such as "I love you," or "Thank you," then we need to say it now before it's too late. Thank God, because of that lesson, I did tell my father and my husband that I loved them every day of my life that they were in my life, just as I say it to my son every day.

I saw myself, during grade school, doing a school project. Each student had to plant and maintain a small garden. I had bought many packets of seeds at the little town hardware store, including one that was called "pot luck." I prepared the area with love and care and then compartmentalized it with pretty borders and colored stones. I tended it daily and lovingly protected it from harm, as if it was a child. The marigold, aster, and daisy seeds yielded those beautiful flowers, predictably, but from the "pot luck" packet came a very disarrayed, disordered disaster. It dawned on me while I was reliving this, that our minds, and for that matter our lives, are just like beautiful gardens to be cherished. We must plant only those positive seeds that will predictably yield beauty, truth, and serenity. That can take self-discipline and courage, no pot luck. We must filter carefully what grows in our space. The harvest we reap springs from those very seeds we plant.

My life review reinforced to me that I have the ability to change my own behavior, but not anyone else's. There have been many times through the years that I've silently let my feelings be hurt by something someone has said. I know now that I have the choice to simply not take those things personally, since in most of the instances that person was dumping his trash on me just because I happened to be there, wrong place, wrong time. The honest excuse that I can make for people who hurt other people with words or deeds is simply this: given that person's previous experiences of his or her lifetime, as well as that person's emotional, intellectual, spiritual, and physical level of maturity, he or she could not have acted any other way at that moment in time. Maturity and new life experiences will bring about more acceptable behavior in their future.

Nietzsche said: "That which doesn't kill us makes us stronger." Reviewing my life showed me my weaknesses, but also my strengths. It reaffirmed to me the fact that we choose how we respond to every second of our lifetime, and that we alone are responsible for those choices.

SEVEN

Changes in Beliefs and Behaviors Following NDEs

Changes that are life-altering often occur as a result of either positive or negative NDEs. These include a decreased fear of death and a renewed belief in life after death, as well as intensified feelings of unconditional love for others; family and friends mean more. It frequently has an impact on the experiencer's religious beliefs, and inspires a feeling of special destiny, or new goals.

The intellect has little to do on the road to discovery. There comes a leap in consciousness, call it intuition or what you will, and the solution comes to you and you don't know how or why.

—Albert Einstein

Benefits of an NDE or LTP

Just as most transcendental NDEs are regarded as a blessing, the LTP experience is also a blessing in disguise because of the significant life-altering changes that occur. They can be a blessing not only to the persons, themselves, but to all of us who study them and experience them vicariously. We can all learn and we can all heal.

I do not mean to imply that it is all roses and clover immediately upon return of the soul into the body. There can be a lot of anger over returning to this earth's reality, there can be overwhelming sadness at leaving the other side if it was a love-filled experience of the bright white God light, and a possible meeting with deceased loved ones. The LTP experiencer can have even more to cope with initially than the NDEr. My LTP cases felt they might automatically be labeled a bad person. We have seen in the accounts presented thus far that once the individual explores (often through therapy) the "why" of the LTP, then suddenly all the dots become connected, a picture forms, and the healing begins. In other words, when experiencers accept where they are now, then they can begin to go forward.

My hypothesis has been that the LTP occurs out of need, a need that is specific to that individual. This might also be said of the transcendental NDEs. Some people only need confirmation that there is a feeling of peace after bodily death. Others require more indepth proof. I have further suggested that the specifics of what one sees, hears, and/or feels in the LTP experience are also determined by that person. If we know what has occurred in their life to that point in time, and also know what their model of the world is (i.e. visual, auditory, or kinesthetic, or a combination of these), then we can predict what the LTP (or NDE) might be. I further hypothesize that any one of us might have the need of an LTP if we need to reevaluate our choices, correct errors in thinking, etc. If we take this one step further, then it is a logical conclusion that if one does their homework, their soul-searching life review now, and resets their compass now, then an LTP might be avoided.

We are all human. None of us is perfect. We learn and grow through the mistakes that we make. If it is true that earth is one gigantic classroom, then we are all here to learn, often by way of those mistakes. We cannot escape our past, the choices we have made, or the actions we have taken. As Viktor Frankl said in *Man's*

Search for Meaning (Simon & Schuster, 1959): "We always have that one final fundamental thing—to choose how we will react to a given situation." We are always in a soul-growth phase. I believe that when the cosmic forces see that we are in need of answers to help us move forward, then we may be given those answers that we might not be privy to in any situation other than an NDE, an LTP, or in deep meditation. That part of our learning experience, our lesson, our karma, we're *shown* in whatever way will impact us via our model of the world. We are shown what we need to see to bring us into harmony with the One (our Creator). NDEs, especially LTPs, remind us that we must take responsibility. They give us permission *not to be perfect*. One should not be complacent after an LTP or an NDE.

NDEs and LTPs may, as we shall see, impact every single aspect of the person's existence, both physical and spiritual. Since we are all connected, that means that every aspect of all of our lives are impacted as well. Lyall Watson, in his book *Lifetide: Biology of the Unconscious* (Simon & Schuster, 1979), described the "100th monkey phenomenon." Japanese researchers studied monkeys in Japan's outer islands for over thirty years. An eighteen-month-old female monkey learned to wash sweet potatoes in the nearby water before eating them. Soon the monkey's mother started doing the same thing, and then she taught it to the other mothers and subsequently to other baby monkeys. At a critical moment a threshold was reached and a new level of awareness seemed to not only be transmitted from the mind of one monkey to another, but actually seemed to jump across the waters to other distant Japanese islands where monkeys suddenly started having the same behavior. Watson suggested that when a certain critical number reaches a particular awareness, it allows for this awareness to break through to become the common consciousness of all. I believe that this is what is happening in the area of Near-Death Experiences. Much of the systematic deafness to important principles and spiritual truths is decreasing, when one is willing to listen to the accounts of these experiences, then the unknown becomes known.

Positive life-altering changes very often occur, both after the typical NDE and after the LTP experience, although these changes can take time to evolve. That's one of the positive things about interviewing a person several months or even years after the experience. It's also helpful when they are reinterviewed months later, and also helpful to confirm those changes by speaking with relatives and friends. I have been blessed to have been able to do just that. Because the changes can be absolutely identical, whether the experience was transcendental or frightening, I will present examples of both. I must admit that even though these wonderful people did not set out to serve as beacons for the rest of the world, that is certainly what they have been to me. Can you tell that I love them all dearly? I feel very grateful and honored that they gave of their time and gave right from their souls and their hearts. Let's see what they have to teach us.

Will Cynics Ever Change Their Minds?

I pray that the cynics among us will not remain spiritually bankrupt, and hope the following fascinating accounts may open some of them up to those higher truths. Cynics have said to me: "Of course a Catholic is going to say he sees Christ, a Buddhist will say he saw Buddha, and a Jew won't see either." Here are two accounts that disprove that statement.

Arnold, sixty-four, is a Jewish gentleman who in his experience not only saw, but was "saved" by Christ. He was kind enough to grant me an interview from the coronary care unit in an Atlanta hospital less than twenty-four hours after his first cardiac arrest, and a second interview within two days of a second episode. He sustained a heart attack leading to the first cardiopulmonary arrest, was resuscitated by paramedics, and taken immediately to a hospital. He underwent a coronary artery bypass (open-heart surgery), during which he had the second episode. I'm happy to say that he has recovered beautifully. I hope to reinterview him again in one year's time to evaluate his long-term life-altering changes. Arnold was raised in a conservative Jewish family. With reference to the first experience he said:

> I was no longer in my body. They were working on me and I was up, up and away! I went through this tunnel and there was Jack! (Arnold's best friend). He pushed me back through this huge door. He gave me a shove like he was saying: "You ain't comin' in this door, Buddy." My damn head almost hit my toes. Then I looked back and my mother and son, both deceased, were standing by the door to make sure. The three of them formed like a line, holding their hands up like when a cop gives you a stop sign at a red light. They kept me far away. They didn't want me close. It was real freaky.

Here is how he described his second experience:

> It was different than the other one. It happened while they were operating [on] me. My heart stopped. I wasn't in a tunnel. Again, my deceased mother and friend were sitting at the bottom of my bed, and they were playing gin! My mother loved action. Know what I'm saying? They were playing gin and then Jesus came walking by! Jesus said to them: "Excuse me," then He picked me up and He said: "I'm going to carry you through this, my son." Do you know *Footprints in the Sand?* Well, I was raised Jewish and am Jewish, and I don't believe in Jesus like the Catholics do. But now I believe in Jesus for Jesus. Understand? He picked me up and said: "I'll carry you through this!"
>
> Jesus put one arm behind my knees and the other arm like under my arms. He was radiant. Radiant! He glowed! He had nice hair, long, brownish, like just barely touching His shoulders. It was a real soothing "Don't worry, my son." His mouth didn't move. He had a beard and mustache and a white sheet-

like shroud, and dark-brown sandals. His hands had long tapered fingers like a piano player. Long fingers, but very strong, yet gentle. I wasn't scared of Him dropping me. He wasn't a real big man, but well built. Real strong, like a carpenter would be. He had the body of a laborer, but the hands of a pianist. I remember that vividly. He looked between 5'10" and 6'. My mother and friend never busted up the game of gin they were playing. He just like very gently swept me up. Blew my mind! Faith is just so strong, if only people would realize that. I can say I'm really blessed now. Imagine, to have my faith tested that way!

Now, my mother and friend never knew each other when they were alive, but my mother liked action. They said: "Yeah, you'll be okay. Just play cards." Then my brother (deceased) came to the foot of the bed and said to me: "When you get through this I want you to keep up with my kids and grandkids." Now, he had died before his grandkids were ever born. I told him I would. He looked just like he did when he was alive. He had died from a heart attack at forty-six.

Ever since my family died so young, I've been forced on a spiritual path. My brother died at forty-six, my father at forty-seven, and my son at twenty-five, all with heart attacks. I was born in 1932. My mother was from the old country. In those days they didn't tell the kids much. When I was in the army and going overseas, my mother said she'd tell me a story. She said when she found out she was pregnant with me, my father had just been turned down for life insurance because he had diabetes and had been wiped out on Wall Street in the Depression because he bought on margin. She had a fourteen-year-old daughter and a seventeen-year-old son, and she was forty and pregnant with me. She didn't want me. She admitted that she wanted to self-abort. She told me that, but she said: "But you came out and you were born at lunchtime, smiling and laughing." And in Yiddish she said to me: "You will have many years that you will live. You have many years. Now, deal the cards!"

I consider myself a truth seeker. When I grew up, most of my friends were Italian. You know, Jews and Italians used to hang. But I never went into a church except maybe Saint Paddy's in New York. When my heart stopped that took all the fear of dying away from me. I say if this is all it is, that's not bad! People need to replace the fear with faith.

I asked Arnold what he thought about the concept of hell. He said:

I think hell is the lowest form of self. The spirit lives. The flesh leaves. You go into a higher plane. I think I'm going to change because of this. My attitude and my priorities will change. What I think is unbelievable is how many people really care for me. Maybe we have less self-worth than we should. If I can be a blessing to someone in their life then what else can you ask for?

Arnold, believe me, you are not only a blessing to me, but to everyone who reads this!

––––––––––

Mona is a Jewish lady who married a Catholic gentleman. Her great-grandfather was a rabbi. Like Arnold, she also had two cardiac arrests. The first one occurred when she was twenty-five years old and pregnant. She went into labor and began hemorrhaging due to a placenta previa. She was taken to surgery, and it was then that the NDE happened.

I was out of my body. Suddenly I was going through a tunnel, like a big circle, all alone, toward this light. I wasn't touching anything. I don't know why, but I wasn't frightened at all. The tunnel ended in an area that was like a regular sand-colored beach. I saw a man in a long robe, the same color as the sand, holding a long wood staff. It was Jesus! He was very tall, six or seven feet, long hair, and a beard. Just His hands were showing. I said to Him: "I'm not ready to go. Please let me go back, I have to raise Barb (her first daughter)." It was all telepathy. I know I wasn't moving my lips, because I didn't think I had lips. He said to me, also without His mouth moving: "I'm going to let you go back. If you're not ready and you don't want to come then I'll send you back." I said to Him: "If you let me live then I'll become a Catholic. I promise." He didn't say anything, but that's when He pushed me back. He sent me back with such a thrust that I still can feel it! I went backward through the tunnel and ended up with a thrust back in my body, all of me at the same time. Since then I was a totally changed person, nothing like the person before. I got more gutsy, much stronger. I didn't tell anyone about it because they'd think I was insane.

The second time I died was two years ago when I was fifty-six. I just didn't feel well. I was in a cardiologist's office to make an appointment to see him for the first time and had a heart attack right then and there! Two doctors and three nurses worked on me to bring me back. They called 911 and put me in ICU. They were going to transfer me to another hospital for the arteriogram (a dye study of the heart arteries) and possibly surgery. I was actually talking to my husband in ICU, getting ready to be transferred, about my funeral plans. I had no fear of death. Now you have to remember that I hadn't kept my word to God. I'd said that I'd convert and I didn't. I asked for a priest and he came. Would you believe the priest did as I asked. He baptized me, confirmed me, and married my husband and me right there, so we'd be married in the eyes of the Church. Then I was transferred to Holy Cross Hospital. All the EKGs at both hospitals, and the ones in the cardiologist's office and in the ambulance, had shown a bad evolving heart attack. All the blood enzymes showed that, too. Right after I was baptized and everything by the priest, I had the cardiac cath. It showed that I had the normal heart of an eighteen year old and the EKG went back to normal!

Many cynics, especially in the scientific fields, say repeatedly that they cannot believe that the person was actually dead because most of the subjects were resuscitated so quickly.

Clarence is a gentleman who was not only dead long enough to make it into a morgue, but dead long enough to be transported to the funeral home! His story is fascinating.

He is now forty-eight years old, and had his telling experience fifteen years ago. Clarence was driving a sixteen-wheeler with his wife as his passenger when another truck hit his truck head-on, killing his wife. He explains:

> It was head-on. All I could do was to just hold on. It drove me and my truck 260 feet down the street backwards. They claimed the other driver was drunk and they charged him with DUI and vehicular homicide. I felt like I went through the windshield and I did, but I was really standing outside the other truck and just walking around. I felt like I had just walked up and seen the wreck. The real me, on the ground, was broke up real bad. When I was walking around I could see through my legs. I mean I could see the ground through my legs. I couldn't feel anything. I tried to touch May, my wife, and it seemed like my hand went through her body. And my truck didn't feel real. I didn't know what was going on. I thought maybe I was hypnotized or something.
>
> In a little while some people came. I was walking around and I heard one say: "Here's the guy that was driving the truck laying right here." I looked, and I seen myself laying there. I kept trying to tell them: "That ain't me. I'm right here!" But didn't nobody hear me. Everything I touched, I reached through. I mean, that was weird! My hand went right through your hand. I tried to shake them (referring to the police on the scene) but they didn't feel me.
>
> May's body was laying there but her spirit, I guess you'd say, was talking to me. She looked like herself. She was telling me it wasn't my fault. I told her: "Well, we'll get out of here. I'll take care of you." We started walking down the road and then I seen the ambulances, and when they came by I seen me and her in the ambulance and I couldn't figure out why we

was in the ambulance when we was walkin' down the road. It was like looking at ghosts.

I could see all the way through May. She kept telling me we'd be all right, that there'd be someone to help us. I told her: "Well, I'm not gonna' leave you." I told her I had to lay down. She said she'd be right there with me and we both laid down and the next time I woke up I was in the county funeral home in Alabama. All I knew was that I was cold and was laying in this room with a bunch of other people. I didn't know why I had no clothes on. I hollered out that I was cold, then a whole bunch of people come in there and they said: "Well, he's not dead, he's talkin'!" They wrapped me up and put me into a helicopter and flew me to Mercy Hospital in Birmingham. Then they told my Mom that I wouldn't be alive in the next three or four minutes if they didn't do brain surgery on me. I had a big blood clot in my brain. I thought I was still in the funeral parlor and I started huntin' for May. I couldn't find her and then I went into a coma.

Clarence remained in a coma for six months, except for one brief period of awakening. He said: "When I finally woke up, I couldn't remember my name or anything else for a while. I didn't even know who my Mama was." I asked Clarence what he remembered of his time in the coma. He said:

I talked to my grandmother and aunt. My grandmother died in 1963 and my aunt died after that. They said they were at the accident. They said it just couldn't be helped and that I shouldn't blame myself. They said May was going to be all right and that they'd take care of her. They were all together. They all had on white dresses. I asked May why she changed her clothes. She said: "Well, we're going back to heaven." They looked like they was walking, but they weren't touching the ground. They was lit up, with light. I seen some stars and clouds. It was like they was walking up into the sky. I didn't want them to go.

I asked Clarence how he felt about religion since the episode. He answered:

> I was raised Baptist. I believe there is a God. I just wish that what happened hadn't happened. He should have left May and just killed me. She had the kids and I don't know nothing about kids. I raised them. Sometimes I wake up talkin' to her and it seems like she's really right there with me. I've seen her several times. She was settin' on the edge of the bed and she's been in the hallway. She's been tryin' to tell me all the times that it's not my fault. She said: "You didn't kill me. It was just an accident."

I asked him if he fears death. His answer was: "No, because I feel like I deserve to die. I wish I could bring May back. After the accident, when I was finally home, I started drinkin' everything I could lay my hands on. I was doin' that to try to forget. But the drunker I get, the worse it gets. I just can't forget!"

I asked Clarence if he had a flashback or a life review. He told me that he did, but the only thing he saw was when he was a five-year-old. He had polio and was having surgery to his legs. It was during that surgery that he had a Near-Death Experience. I asked him to tell me everything he could remember about it. He said:

> I was five. I seen them doing surgery on my legs in the operating room. I knew it was me. I was watching from the ceiling. I had a very high temperature. They were saying that they didn't know if the vaccine would help or not. I remember a light that was real bright, but it was like in a pipe or something. It looked like it was a long ways away from where I was. I remember it well, even though it was so long ago. I went in and tried to find out where the light was comin' from, but I couldn't go that far. I came back out. I heard: "Don't worry, you'll be okay. You'll make it. We'll take care of your legs. Go back down there and let them finish." It was a man's voice, but it was real soft. It made you feel safe. I felt love, and I felt if I do what it says I'll be all right. So I turned around

and crawled back out. I was paralyzed from the waist down until I was thirteen and then it got where I could walk again.

My next question was difficult. I asked why he felt that God allowed him to live after the accident. His answer:

> I don't know, because if I was Him I would have let me die and kept her alive. She never did nothin' to nobody and I've always acted crazy. My Mama said God left me here for a reason, but I don't know what it could be. I don't know what I could do to help somebody, as great as He is. I'm nothin' and He's everything. If I could wish for one thing and have it come true it'd be to be there. If the good Lord has something for me to do here, I wish He'd hurry up and let me know.

Clarence raised his children with his mother's help. He has completed a full twenty-eight-day alcohol rehabilitation treatment program and is extremely active with Alcoholics Anonymous. He speaks very often at those meetings about all that he has been through and what he has learned. He has brought comfort to many. He has been a great help to many people going through the grieving process after losing a loved one. He now sees it as a great blessing (which we discussed at great length) that his wife May continues to watch over him and their children. He now feels certain that, when it is his time to join her, she will be waiting to help him "cross over."

Frequently Seen Life-Altering Changes Following NDEs and LTPs

The most statistically significant life-altering change in my study is decreased fear of death. Of course the circumstances leading up to the death, such as metastatic cancer of the bone, can certainly be very painful. The data shows that 76.8 percent of the NDErs have a deceased fear of death as a direct result of their brush with death, as compared with 63.4 percent of the LTP experiencers. Several reasons account for such a high percentage of decreased death fears with people who had frightening experiences. I believe that the main reason is that they had confirmation at death that the soul continues to have an existence, even after the physical body dies. Many people had an out-of-body experience immediately after an accident and, therefore, did not feel the pain that the physical body was experiencing. Upon return to the body, the pain, of course, was felt.

Many of the people whom I interviewed have stopped attending funerals. They tell me it is not out of disrespect, but rather because they now know that the deceased person still exists on the other side. When the Near-Death Experience is profoundly mystical, with the feeling of unconditional love and joy, there is a wonderful peace in knowing that their loved one is "home" and happy.

56.6 percent of NDErs and 67.7 percent of the Less-Than-Positive experiencers have an increased belief in life after death. NDEs and LTPs also impact tremendously on one's religious belief. Most experiencers say that, although they have less interest in organized religion, both groups of people are more religious and more spiritual. Nearly everyone's belief in God is increased. People who considered themselves to be agnostic or atheistic before the experience do not remain so. They say that not only do they know that God does exist, but that He is a loving, kind, nonjudgmental God, the One God. The data shows that 51 percent of the NDErs said that their episode significantly impacted on their religious beliefs. 58.3 percent of the LTP experiencers responded positively as well.

The bottom line with all of these experiences is love: love of family, love of friends, love of humanity. NDErs, especially those who have had deep core experiences, have an inner peace and contentment. They try not to allow pain, worry, or hatred to enter their hearts because their hearts are already overflowing with love.

Of the NDErs who came back from the other side, 43.8 percent returned with a feeling of special importance, or feeling that they had a special destiny; 41.7 percent of the Less-Than-Positive experiencers were similar, and 25.5 percent of the NDErs knew, specifically, what their new goals were, as did a significant 44.4 percent of the LTP people. Those people now feel empowered to live with zest and fulfill their purpose for this lifetime. These life-altering changes are but a few of the blessings in disguise of the LTP experiencer. The following accounts will illustrate these points.

———————

Bonnie, when in her twenties, was among the first hundred women to go to Japan after World War II. She was an artist, commissioned to paint murals on the service men's clubs. She was bitten by a monkey, went into a coma, and was hospitalized in an army hospital. She said:

> I heard them pronouncing me dead. Suddenly, the side of the hospital room opened up and there I was going up this long tunnel. While I was in the tunnel I saw something in my past. When I was in college I visited my best friend and went off with her cousin in a speedboat to go dancing. Everyone was very worried because they didn't know where we had gone. I saw my best friend's mother in the flashback, and she was very worried. Then I saw a brilliant light and there was fantastic music. I heard a voice. It was a deep, gentle, soft, resonant voice, not demanding. It said: "The greatest sin is to hurt another human being." Then it said: "Do you want to come with me?" I said: "No, I want to stay." That's when they resuscitated me. I had never told anyone about this.
>
> I know it was me who made the decision to return. Sometimes I regret it. I'm not afraid of death. As a matter of fact, there are times that I would welcome it. I think when someone is terminal then Dr. Kevorkian is doing humanity a service. We do it to our dogs and horses when they're suffering, why shouldn't we do it to our humans when they're suffering? It's just the suffering body that ceases to exist, not the spirit. We still live after the body dies.

———————

David, a long time medical patient of mine, was brought up Catholic. He was the only remaining child after his brother died as a youth. His parents, also my patients, became very ill in their later years. David was their loving sole caregiver until the time they each went into their spirit form. That was his special destiny and the reason why he was allowed to return from death in Vietnam.

In Vietnam I was caught in an explosion of a rocket. It picked me up and threw me sixty feet. It left me unconscious. I heard a hum and then I was above my body. I was witnessing what was going on, and I think it was during that period that they, whoever they are, were trying to determine whether I was staying or going. I was looking down at my body and then I heard a high-pitched sound. I looked off to my right, through what I thought was a window. I saw a very bright light, like rays of light. It was almost blinding, but my eyes adjusted right away. Then I saw figures. One was dressed in white. I thought I saw Abraham and I thought I saw Michael, the Archangel. He had wings, and he was bigger than life! When he saw you, he saw your soul. It was electrifying to the soul. I think it was Michael who said: "It may or may not be your time. Patience for a moment."

I was shown a lot of things that happened in my life, including things that happened in Vietnam. I saw when I was out on a long patrol with a major who I was best friends with. As we walked through a mountain passage we were ambushed and he got shot. He was three feet away from me. A battle ensued between three of us and about six of them. Five of them died. One was shot in the knee. His gun jammed. I walked over to him and assassinated him. That's what I saw. It brought back tremendous pain. I thought I'd have to pay penance the rest of my life. He was only wounded in the knee but I shot him in the head with my .45. I put three shells into his head. I was so angry that my friend died next to me, that I killed four people that day. That is the cross I live with. It could've been a self-imposed judgment that I felt. Something told me it was wrong. I knew I would have to do something to try to make up for this, because no man has a right to do what I did.

When I was seeing my life, I also saw people dressed like in the fifties and sixties. I felt a kinship and friendship to them. I saw the funeral of my brother. I was only eighteen months old then. Mom had to put him in a pauper's grave. I saw my aunt coming into the house to buy some of my mother's things and take them out, so Mom would have money to bury my brother. I saw myself when I was four. I was falling down a hill and sliding under a bridge and going for a hundred yards, and stopped five feet from a cliff. I was shown that I was stopped for a reason.

I think that some of the figures I saw in the light were my family. I think one was my baby brother. He died as a baby, but now he has grown up. Another was an uncle who I loved with all my heart. I felt a true kinship to them. Then I felt like a hand give me a push on my back, and that literally threw me back into my body. The pain was excruciating from my injuries.

I asked David what changes he feels he has undergone because of his NDE. He said:

Death doesn't faze me. I know I have a job to do here. Actually, most of the job was to take care of my parents. I honestly feel that everything I was supposed to do for myself I must have done in a previous life. Now I have to do for others. I was brought up in a very religious family. Now I don't feel like I have to go to church, because I feel like my church is with me all the time. I really feel like I have a guiding light over me.

David also said that he has now come to terms with what happened in Vietnam.

————

Juliana is in her forties. She had an experience when she was in a deeply meditative state. She and her two sons, who are also very spiritual, have come to many of the South Florida IANDS meetings. She said:

> I became separate from my body. I went into the light, astral light, God's light. I felt connected to the light. I felt I was being reborn. The old is gone. After this type of experience you have to come back to an earthly balance. But, honestly, when I was in that state I saw no purpose to life at all. This physical life seemed so trite. I lost my fear of death, because I see it as just another door, the beginning of something else. I know that death is not the end. There is an afterlife. That much I did find out.
>
> Even now, my mother is dying and it's making me accept it and understand that she's going to be okay. She'll be better off, because she won't have that body that's giving her so much trouble. She's going to be fine, and she'll be there, somewhere. When you have contact with those who have departed, then you know there is another side. And, obviously, they can come down to earth to help when we're in need of help. Is it an angel? Who knows? It doesn't matter what you call it. I see death and life the same. When you die, it's just like being reborn.
>
> They say "know yourself and you will know all," because it is all within you. So when you meditate, you need to go within. It is definitely not an intellectual exercise. You are more than your physical body. You almost have to get out of your body to realize that. It's like Socrates said: "I'm still here! I am not my body." You can chop my legs and my arms off and I'm still here. If there's nothing left but my spirit, it's still me! I've realized that we're all just in costume. My body is my physical facade that I present to everyone. Once you have this type of experience you don't see any differences in people, no matter what the color of their skin is. We are all one. We're all part of the same family, from the same origin.

I feel that meditation, like Maslow's vertical exodus, is going up in your state of consciousness. We are the microcosm within the macrocosm. All the knowledge of all time and all wisdom is within us. And I know it is all from God.

Paige was fifty-six years old when she had a stroke. She said she was in bad shape when she arrived in the emergency room.

The priest anointed me. I had a stroke before I ever got to the hospital and then I stroked again in the emergency room and they called a "code blue." The ceiling seemed to open and I saw heaven. There were only two people there: my husband, who had passed away, was in a white robe, and he was sitting next to Jesus. They were sitting on a yellow brick wall, around three feet high, that had a white cap on top of it. I raised my hand toward the Lord. He bent over and put his hand down, so His hand was about six feet away from mine. He was the most beautiful man in the world. His complexion was olive color and His cheeks were rosy. His nose was very, very straight. His jaw line was very defined and perfect, as though it was carved or chiseled. In my opinion, He had a mixture of racial colors. I could see where He could be called black, and I could see where He would be called American Indian and I could see oriental. He had gorgeous long flowing chestnut-brown hair, no beard. My husband still had his beard that was very neatly groomed, as he always kept it.

When Jesus put his hand down, like to reach toward mine, my husband put his hand down and pushed Jesus' hand away from mine and he said: "Jesus, don't do that." Jesus said: "Why not?" All this time my hand was up there pleading, because I wanted to get in so bad. It had just seemed like Jesus was going to pull me up off the stretcher. So my husband told Jesus that my daughter couldn't handle it if I came there so soon after his passing, that she was unstable and that would make her worse. Jesus said: "You're probably right." I was horrified! I couldn't believe it! Ergo, I didn't get into heaven. I wasn't too thrilled because I knew I was going to be in for a bad time here on earth. I was angry, to tell you the truth. That's the story in a nutshell.

I asked Paige if she could further describe Jesus. We can tell by her descriptions that she is a very visual and artistic person. She said:

Jesus' hands were very long. He was dressed in a white robe up to the neck, down to the floor, and the sleeves were down to the wrists. It seemed like a satin material, like my husband's robe. I didn't see Jesus' eyes. I'm sure that if I did, then I wouldn't have been able to come back. I'm an eye person. I didn't see His teeth. I just saw a side and partial frontal view of His face. He only spoke to my husband, not to me. His voice was very mellow and soothing. It wasn't loud or thunderous. It was a real loving voice. He sounded like a father talking to a child that's old.

It wasn't what I expected at all. I didn't see anyone else up there. I found it hard to believe that my dad, my grandmother, and other people I know who had led such holy lives weren't there. I thought I'd see a whole bunch of people mulling around up there.

I should tell you about the light. It wasn't a blinding light like I've read about. It was like the light you'd see through an airplane window when you look down at the clouds. It was just white, all white. Everything up there was white. The inside of heaven looks like a white, fluffy cloud. I didn't see any gold or any angels. All I saw was Jesus and my husband. My husband acted and looked just the same as when he was here. Can you imagine? He was telling Jesus what to do! It was very quiet up there, but it won't be when I get there! That's probably why Bill didn't want me up there.

I asked Paige how she's changed because of the experience and if she feels that she got what she needed from the event. She said:

I have changed because of it, for the better. I'm making more of an effort to make brownie points to get into heaven.

I figure this is probably purgatory. I don't get in up there until I suffer more than I have. I have to do penance here before I die. But believe me, I'm not afraid to die any more. I welcome it with open arms. I just hope I get a good place up there.

I surely did get what I needed from that experience. It made me accept the paralyzed condition that I'm in. It made me accept it better because I'm sure it has to be for a good reason. I'm going to act as an example to my grandkids of how you carry a cross and accept your bad breaks in life without letting them get to you. And now when I look at people, I look for the good in them. There is good in all of us, one way or the other.

———————

Doris not only lost her fear of death, but now says that she has confirmation of an afterlife. She became much more religious after her NDE, and has demonstrated some healing abilities. Like many other experiencers, she was very depressed upon return from the other realm. She had quite a unique experience, in which she became a lovely bird in flight after her soul separated from her body.

Now it's four years that has passed. It was our fiftieth wedding anniversary. We had just moved to Florida so we could become active in the large Presbyterian Church. Our families came down from Atlanta for the anniversary party. I fell in the hall and was rushed to the hospital. Dr. Jose Diaz saved my life! My leg was broken badly and shattered near my hip. I had fallen so hard that I hemorrhaged and nearly died, or maybe did die. I had to have blood transfusions.

I had a life and death experience. I know it was not a dream. I had become a bird, and was with another bird. We were so high in the sky that we couldn't see the tops of the trees! Behind us there was nothing but darkness. As in scripture, I'll say that God's voice spoke to me. In front of us there was heaven's door and a huge light. I said to my friend: "There are five others over there just going through the door.

I wonder if they are someone we know." Then there was God's word that came to me and He said: "Darkness is in the past. Darkness does not have the last word, light does. Despair does not have the last word, hope does. Death does not have the last word, life does." Then I wondered what the meaning of the bird was. I knew I was at peace and I wanted to go through that door. I was just as free as a bird. We were all heading toward the light and heaven's door. I kept looking at the light and wanting to go through that door. I had such peace! Just as we were getting near it, I came to as a nurse was saying to me: "Doris, you are not going to die. You are going to live," and I had been so ready to go through to the light.

When I came home I was very ill. I never knew what depression was until then. I never used to cry, but I cried and cried for so long. But in all the days of suffering I never doubted that the Lord was with me. He was there to hold my hand and always talk to me. I always felt His presence. Now I know there are so many reasons why God wanted me to live. It's funny, but the day I arrived home, so very depressed, I turned on the TV to the spiritual network, and the first thing I heard was a song about the dove with a broken wing. It just seemed that song was meant for me and it gave me hope.

I do realize that my work isn't finished. I visited a friend recovering in a nursing home. We had prayed over her and she was healed from her cancer. I choose to believe there is no end to this story. It will just go on and on and on. As I was telling my husband the other day, we are not married for death do us part, we are married for eternity.

God is not asking for us for our abilities, it is our availability. We are all called but not everyone answers. There's no little people or big people. He loves us all the same. We all have some gift. Some people have several gifts. Maybe my gift is a small gift, like loving my neighbor. We all have a different calling. Yours is different. Your work is your gift.

Jeanne R., now seventy years old, is a gentle soul. I feel very blessed that she is my medical patient. She has had four Near-Death Experiences! Besides this, there are other reasons why her accounts are unusual. She came back healed of cancer (leiomyosarcoma) after the third experience. The fourth NDE was also atypical because for three days she went back and forth to the astral plane, and when she returned for the final time she was healed of mycoplasma pneumonia.

> I was sixteen when the first one happened. I was having surgery for endometriosis. Suddenly I shot out of my body to over the operating table and then I was in a tunnel, on my back, just inching along slow motion toward the light at the end. It was just this intense, intense bright white light. The tunnel was only big enough for me. I was alone, and there weren't any sounds, and I remember a lack of color. I don't know what interrupted it, but I came back into my body. The next one happened when I was in college, having abdominal surgery again. Really, the exact same thing happened.
>
> In 1964 was the third experience. I had a hysterectomy and had a cancer, a leiomyosarcoma, which had spread. They told my family I had up to three months to live. They didn't tell me, but I found out later, because I ended up healed of that cancer and it had to have been because of the Near-Death Experience. It really wasn't much different than the other two, though. I had the out of body, the tunnel, and the light. But the light was such a pure white light, so intense that I can't describe it. It was magnetic. I felt it was drawing me. The closeness I felt to God when I came back and even now is unreal.
>
> Then in 1984, after my second husband died, I was so sick with pneumonia that I had to be hospitalized. This experience was totally different from the other three. I went out of my body, but I ended up standing on a hillside. I was looking down a gentle slope to a little stream that was no more than three steps across. There was a little wood bridge going across. On the other side was my husband, dead less than a year, my

father, and my mother's parents. It was sort of like a welcoming committee. They wanted me to come and I wanted to go, but failed.

We had conversations across the stream for three days. Their mouths didn't open, but I heard what they were saying in my head. As I kept getting closer to the little crossing on the bridge, I was obviously getting closer to death. I still resent coming back, like God, how can you fail dying? You know the old cliché about your work isn't done yet, well, that just doesn't cut it!

I asked Jeanne to describe any changes she feels she's had since the NDEs and to comment upon the reason or reasons why she was sent back.

That state of being is pure love and peace and joy. If only people on earth could experience it, then there would be no war. There'd be nothing but a happy humanity. When you've been there, you can help somebody else, which I couldn't do if I hadn't worn those shoes. I run a grief support group and I'm a caregiver. Every day I thank God for my day. I hope that whatever I do that day, that I've made it a little better for someone else. That's why I'm here. Everything in my life now is an open book, and I feel that's where I help people, because I can listen and they know that I've been there. So my phone rings all day. It's neat to be able to open my soul to other people. That's what I'm about. I don't judge anybody. I used to be cautious, but now who cares? Go for it girl! You only go around once, so don't miss a thing. And over there you learn the value of love. I'm a hugger. What matters most is people, love and people, and helping people to know what love is all about. And I told you about the closeness I feel to God. We just pal around together all the time now.

Brenda, another medical patient, is also a cancer survivor. In 1988, in her thirties, within a three-week period she had two operations for metastatic ovarian cancer. Her experience impacted on her tremendously, especially spiritually. She has not only lost her fear of death, but her other fears as well.

The second operation was very lengthy. They found tumors invading the diaphragm. In removing them, they nicked the diaphragm so that both lungs collapsed, following which I developed pneumonia and was on a respirator. I became very, very ill. One night I got really sick. Everybody came rushing into the room with all kinds of equipment and stuff. I was in a room on the special gynecological oncology (cancer) unit and I had private RNs around the clock. I remember all the doctors working on me. Everything hurt. I could hear my family pleading with me to fight. Everything hurt, and they were in so much pain, themselves. They rolled me over and put chest tubes in my back. I was screaming, and then suddenly I was no longer in the bed. I was watching the team of doctors and nurses and all the machines from above. I remember leaving, like a total checkout. The room seemed almost miniature, like a very small square, in black and white. I went from all this pain to no pain and nothing.

Before that I knew I was Jewish, but I never believed in God. I still have no strong religious beliefs. I believe more now in trust of self, in who I am as a human being. My higher being is the person I was created to be. I believe there are higher beings and that adds a dimension to who we are. I remember when the nurses would come in when I was in the hospital, and they would pray. I thought to myself: "How can I ever get through this without that kind of strength like they have in their religious beliefs?" But then later I found that my higher power is within me. That was the turning point in my survival. It was the change in my spirituality, and changing from a dying sense to a living sense, that made the color return.

What matters most is just living and learning that the things you thought were so important really have so little meaning. Even the things at work that I was so frantic about are foolish, as are my fears. I was afraid of flying, and that's the biggest joke of all! All those stupid fears have just gone away. I'm much closer to my family. They count. One of those experiences just puts everything in perspective.

———————

Willie Mae has been my medical patient for many, many years. Close to twenty years ago she tried to tell me about her Near-Death Experience. I guess I just wasn't totally open then. I didn't see her for several years because of a change of insurance at her work. She returned when I was beginning the research on NDEs. There are no accidents! Everything really does happen just exactly as it is supposed to. Willie Mae has taught me so very much. What a true blessing she has been in my life. Her spirituality and psychic abilities increased a thousand-fold after the event.

> When I had my tonsils out when I was twenty-three, I went through something hollow at warp speed. There were some people in there that didn't have any form. When I got to the end I could see the stars, and there was a man and a lady. I knew they loved me. I believe the young man was Christ. He wouldn't talk. There was a glow, brighter than sunlight, and there was beautiful music. There was a lit-up city of lights. There were huge buildings, with, like, windows all lit up, with the beautiful color of transparent purple behind them.
>
> Those stars in the universe are lights, energy, because it has been proven that power is nothing but energy. Those stars that come out aren't just being pretty in the universe. Those stars, I believe, are places the souls can go.

I asked Willie Mae what she feels is the reason for our existence on this earth plane. Many times through the years she has seen my son, Willy, at my office. As I previously explained, he has many sensory deficits including blindness and decreased hearing. His motor skills are impaired because of cerebral palsy. He is also mentally retarded and cannot speak. That little boy is purity, personified. He doesn't have an aggressive bone in his body. His smile and his laugh lights up a room, as it lights up my life. Because I know that many of you have children with developmental challenges, I shall share with you what Willie Mae said about my Willy (and about me):

> I believe we are here to love. I believe we have to experience every race in order that we will learn to love everybody. First you have to learn to love yourself, and then you can love everyone else. But if you haven't learned the art of loving yourself then you'll never love anyone. I believe that we eventually become a male and a female and a member of every race. And I believe we even go through experiencing homosexuality in order to understand that.
>
> I believe that your son, Willy, was put in that body to experience it so that he could tell the next person in the next life about it. The real person within that body really has every part of a normal body. His spirit body has eyes that can see, feet that can walk, ears that can hear, and a mouth that can speak. He's really a whole person, but this is what we see and touch. It's what we can't see that is real. This whole world is really an illusion. Your son, Willy, came in like that to teach you and your husband and himself. God is not the perpetrator. God wants us to experience in order to have more compassion for other people and to understand that we are subject to the same body if we don't get our act together. If you hadn't had the son that you did, maybe you wouldn't have had the amount of compassion that you have.

I asked Willie Mae if she feared death and what she thinks happens after one dies.

> This body doesn't die. It's a transporter. But there is something within that's the real person. After you become deceased I think you can take on many forms. I don't visit funeral homes any more because I know they're not there, that is, not in their bodies. They're watching you watching them. To me, they're like in an arena, saying: "What are you doing down there?"

I believe that there are other worlds and when you've progressed enough, you go higher. You keep going and going until you perfect yourself. You keep coming back until you're perfect.

Willie Mae said about me:

Dr. Rommer, I tried to tell you years ago that you were chosen, but you weren't ready. You have to let people know that there is life after death and you have to hurry. I was sent to tell you that you are an old woman of wisdom (I was forty at the time). You have to tell people that it's all right to die. It's all right. Everything is all right. Like a counselor, you have to tell the people that it's all right to cross over. You're helping them to make it over. You medically work on the internal organs, and the spiritual side is that you are working for the soul in order to get them where they have to go, like a medium. I can feel the energy and healing that you channel. It took you years, but you're there now.

Willie Mae came to a South Florida IANDS meeting, and shared a lot of her wisdom with us. She said: "Many of you came because you are afraid to die. Don't ever be afraid. Dying is the beginning."

——————

Patrick had a spiritually transforming event in 1993, when he was forty-one. He had already been on a spiritual quest, which brought him to Delphi where we met when we were taking courses on mediumship. His NDE experience proves that even if it is brief, it can be quite life-altering. He said:

I had attended the deactivation of a nuclear submarine in Fort Lauderdale at the invitation of the then-captain of the sub, a long-time, close, personal friend. The dock area was secured. We were permitted access only via a chartered bus. As I was stepping off the bus, with one foot on the pavement of this horseshoe-shaped parking lot, a vehicle raced by, doing at least forty miles per hour, and sideswiped me, running over my

foot. I was suddenly away, in a peaceful and suspended state, as calm as the eye of a storm. Time was stopped. Then, as quickly as it occurred, the suspended state disappeared and I was back hearing all the screaming, because everyone thought I was hurt.

That brief episode changed my life. I realized that there are definite purposes for me being here. I would not have understood the magnitude of the incident had I not already been involved in spiritual development, on a quest.

We don't die. The physical body is merely a vessel that we temporarily occupy for the purpose of working out the lessons and dealing with life's circumstances that are presented on this plane. It's like if you rent a car for a trip. When you finish the trip you return the car, and when it's time to take another trip, you rent another car. They used to say there's only two things, death and taxes. Well, I've narrowed it down to taxes. You don't die, you just transition. Of course there's sadness at someone's death, because they're not physically here for you to touch. But if you live on the East Coast and call an aunt that lives in California on the phone, you're not physically touching her either. When someone dies, they're also just a long distance phone call away!

Bess was in her twenties when she had her Near-Death Experience. It had some features of a Less-Than-Positive experience. She had also had a cardiac arrest as an infant, and feels that it was the direct cause of her increased psychic abilities. Through the years she has had many significant medical problems to deal with, including cancer, multiple skin and brain tumors (known as neurofibromatosis), and a seizure disorder. Any one of these might test a person's faith. Bess admits that prior to her LTP experience she labeled herself an atheist. She has had astounding spiritual growth and, with time, has demonstrated many life-altering changes which she attributes to that experience. With reference to the immediate changes, she said: "I stopped drugs, stopped dancing and partying, changed friends, and am no longer an atheist." She also said that the LTP experience was exactly what she needed to bring about those changes.

I had to be hospitalized. I had been doing drugs and took too many. It was kind of intentional, I must admit, because I just wanted to go to sleep. Luckily I called a friend and told her what I'd done. I was on a gurney in the middle of the hallway and all of a sudden I heard a hum and was over my body looking at myself. I remember the nurse saying: "We're losing her!" They tried to stick a tube down my throat. I started convulsing. In a couple of seconds I felt calm, an utter peace. I looked to my right, above my shoulder, and the corner got really, really long and there was a beautiful light at the end of it. I was drawn there.

At the end of this tunnel was my aunt who had died. She was young-looking, beautiful, draped in this beautiful thing, and was just smiling and inviting me. She emulated light and hope. She was standing at these big double doors, about three feet away. There was the wonderful light on both sides of her. I think if I had gone over to where she was, I would not have come back. Then I felt a force behind me, pulling me back. Did you ever go over a bump and your stomach falls? I said: "Please, please, I want to stay. Don't take me back." Whatever this thing was behind me, it was powerful, almost touching me, pulling me back. It was like a suction! I was sucked back into my body, my ass first, right into my groin area, and then the rest of my body came in. The next thing I knew I woke up on the machines in ICU. The nurse was shaking me, but I slipped back into the tunnel and saw lots of faces of people that I didn't know. Some were scary and some were calm. There were over a hundred faces. They went by in a split second. I saw this one man who had on a brimmed hat, older, skeleton-looking—meaning thin and hollowed out. I remember a fat guy, portly, bald all around. I also saw a young girl with blond hair down to her back playing. The people didn't have bodies, just faces, and they were wearing, like, bathrobes. I did that three times, the same thing, with the faces.

I saw all of that because that's what God wanted me to see. For a while I was an atheist. When I was twenty I was diagnosed with this disease and cancer and I was really pissed off. I was going through a pretty hard time. I was a cynic. I felt there was no God. Maybe this experience was to show me that there really is something after. Maybe it was to restore my faith in God, the spirits, and angels.

I flatlined when I was a baby. I was apparently born with cancer. My lungs collapsed. I went into respiratory failure and flatlined at fourteen days old. Maybe that's why I have the things I have today. I dream about things that end up happening just as I have dreamed. I can see auras. I can make people feel better when they're ill. And with a lot of people I can see them as children and see in flashes what happened to them, like in the movies. I can see parts of their childhood, and a lot of it is bad. It doesn't seem like I see the good things. I can see like their inner being. I have had many experiences where I have seen spirits.

I had another Near-Death Experience when I was sick one time. I just saw a light, no tunnel, and golden hills. I went up this mountain that was gold and purple, just beautiful. My aunt was on top. The wind was blowing and she looked like an angel in typical angel dress, white and flowing. She had hands but a transparent body. She didn't have a body or feet, but you could tell by how everything was blowing that it was blowing through a nonbody. But she definitely had a face and hair and was my aunt. I also saw water, a valley, and ancient ruins that looked like Athens, Greece. It was beautiful. I think it was a waiting station, like before heaven.

I asked Bess why she feels she had the experiences and how else she has changed because of them.

I stopped drugs and partying. I got away from those people and situations. I just think God was saying: "Hey, wake up and smell the coffee. You have this life to live." I'm much more sympathetic to others now. I think that's why God let me have this gift. Sometimes I do have seizures, or my back hurts, or I look at my face and see all those bumps, and see the scar on my stomach. I think God was saying to me: "Well, there's more to you than just your looks. It's what's inside that counts." It made me work on what I am inside, to be a nicer and kinder human being. That's one of the reasons I had the experiences.

To the question: "Why are we here?" she answered:

Everyone's here for a different reason, whether it's to make a mark to make a difference in the world, or to have lots of children, or maybe to teach someone else a lesson whether it's good or bad. Even bad people, like [Ted] Bundy, may have been sent here for that reason. I don't want to say that God would make someone that evil, but I think He lets life take its course. I used to think how could there be a God if He lets all these evil things happen? Then, after I had the NDE, I thought maybe He doesn't make it happen but He just lets it happen. He lets life run its course for other people to learn so other people can understand pain, so they'll learn the reality of a forgiving God. God forbid something like murder happened to someone I really love, but I think you learn from your pain and mistakes. And there comes a peace afterwards. When I got sick I always wondered why? But now I think the sickness made me a stronger person.

I asked Bess what she thinks about organized religion.

If you have God or a Higher Power, it's good. I don't believe in organized religion per se, in following the rules. I just think you must believe in something higher than you, whether Allah, Buddha, or whoever. I don't necessarily believe Jesus is the son of God. I do believe He was a prophet and did walk the earth. I've studied a lot of religions. I do believe everyone has a guardian angel, or I wouldn't be alive.

I have to tell you something that will amaze you as a physician. When I was first diagnosed with the tumors, I had three of them in my brain. I got blessed by a reverend and my mom took me to a medicine man of the Seminole tribe. When the MRI was repeated after that it only showed two tumors, not three, and the two were shrunk. You know how unusual that is, 'cause usually they either grow or stay stagnant.

My philosophy is that I envision a stairway throughout our life. Each stair is a triumph. When we die, if we have more steps to take, then we come back. Speaking of death, I certainly don't fear it. It's wonderful!

Marilyn had a Type I Less-Than-Positive Near-Death Experience. You will recall that the Type I LTP is described just the same as an illuminating one, but the person perceives it as frightening. At thirty-four years old, Marilyn developed severe thrombocytopenia (decreased platelets, which assist in clotting), kidney failure, and she had to have dialysis. She feels that she came back with a "significant message to spread."

I was in the hospital in bad shape. Blood started pouring out of my nose, mouth, ears, and every orifice. My brother flew in to see me, dressed in his funeral suit. The lady from the dietary department was talking to me about the menu and, all of a sudden, I couldn't understand her. I was just floating away, and suddenly I was in this dark place. I was floating forward, vertically. I was fascinated by it. The walls were billowing in and out, almost like smoke. I put my hand through the side of it, and there was nothing there. Then it dawned on me that I remembered reading *Life After Life* (by Dr. Raymond Moody) and remembered the description of the tunnel and knew what was happening. I had never taken it seriously, because I've always been a skeptic. Then I thought: "Oh, my God, I'm going!" I was terrified! I had thoughts going through my head, like maybe I should have stayed with the

Fundamentalists. Then all of a sudden I knew that if I came back it would be harder than if I went forward. But I made the choice to come back, and when I did I felt myself being sucked backwards very, very fast. Any doubt that there's life after death has been erased from my mind. I saw the movie *Resurrection*, and it scared me to death because it was so close to what I had experienced.

We're here to love one another and to be as much like Christ as possible. The purpose of life is to love one another unconditionally. When I start to get irritated with people, I remind myself that I'm not doing what I'm here to do. Religion has put a lot of fear in me that wasn't necessary. I know that the Christians would probably be upset with me, but I just don't think they have a monopoly on heaven. I think that people who have had a Near-Death Experience have a message to spread: that love thy neighbor is the main thing. Love them unconditionally.

––––––––––

Learning to love one another unconditionally does seem to be a bottom line with these experiences. We can choose to see the ugliness in another or we can choose to see God within him. What we see in another is really a mirror image of ourselves. We are all a part of each other. We can choose to see the beauty, as we can choose to walk in light and not get stuck in the ugliness. We are not here to fix the world or save the world, but to love it just the way it is. It and everyone in it is worthy of unconditional love. May we remember that, and not need a Near-Death Experience or Less-Than-Positive Experience to remind us.

EIGHT

Psychic and Spiritual Gifts, Changes in Values and Beliefs

My research shows that increased psychic ability is a common occurrence following a Near-Death Experience. This is very subjective. Testing was not done to prove or disprove the subject's psychic abilities, but I was certainly impressed with what I consider to be evidence of increased clairvoyance, clairsentience, and other psychic abilities. In answer to the question: "Do you believe that your psychic abilities have increased since your experience?" 38.4 percent of the Near-Death experiencers and 41.2 percent of the Less-Than-Positive experiencers whom I interviewed felt that their psychic abilities increased dramatically.

Many of these people are now devoting their lives to spiritual counseling, channeling information from the other side, and doing psychic investigations. In this chapter are transcripts of interviews with several subjects

Do not follow where the path leads. Rather, go where there is no path and leave a trail.

—Anonymous

who are now doing work in this area. Some who have a true ability to heal others always state that they are "merely the channel through which the Higher Power heals." Many have prophetic visions, and the majority of the most psychically gifted people I have met are those who had multiple Near-Death Experiences. The incidents almost seemed additive, one building upon another. If we were to painstakingly study this group, I believe we would find that true clinical death was involved in every case. I studied their medical records whenever possible, but sometimes the records weren't available because the event had occurred too many years ago.

I spent many weeks at Delphi, in the Blue Ridge Mountains of Georgia, taking courses in mediumship and spiritual healing in order to sharpen my own psychic abilities for the purpose of more in-depth interviewing for this study. I did some of my most fascinating interviews there with intuitives (another name for psychics).

Many of those interviewed have increased the amount of reading that they do (50 percent of the LTP experiencers and 32 percent of the NDErs). Many not only tend to read now about other people's NDEs and other metaphysical material, but read more in general. Their thirst for knowledge isn't just for the sake of knowledge, but in search of wisdom; often a direct result of the information gained on the other side. Others are seeking answers that they weren't privy to. Most are on a true spiritual quest.

Changes in values and beliefs after an NDE or LTP are common; 44.4 percent of the LTP experiencers noted these changes, as compared with 33.9 percent of the NDErs. In large part, this had to do with the impact of the experience on their religious beliefs. In fact, belief in reincarnation frequently increases after an experience; a few people said that something specific in the experience confirmed for them that reincarnation occurs. Those few people did have a review of either a previous lifetime or a future lifetime. (Please refer back to Wesley's story in chapter two.) Carole Sanborn Langlois, author of

Soul Rescue (That's the Spirit Pub., 1993), told me she believes that even if the person doesn't feel there is anything specific in their experience that confirms reincarnation for them, the NDE "awakens a remembrance of the soul of other past lives."

It is not surprising that 58.3 percent of the LTP experiencers say they have literally changed how they live their lives, and 29.6 percent of the NDErs also affirmed this. Every single aspect of one's life can be affected. Decreased interest in and obsession with material things (including decreased interest in wealth "for the sake of wealth") is frequently reported. The interviews in this chapter were all very intense for the experiencers and caused them to undergo most of these (and other) life-altering changes.

It should already be obvious that the depth and seeming length of an NDE or LTP experience is not a good predictor of the life-altering changes that will occur. A "short" episode that consists of an out-of-body experience (as occurring with an accident), then a moment of darkness, followed by a "partial" trip through a tunnel, may cause more than just a few long-term aftereffects. A deep core experience, where the subject meets with deceased relatives or guides, is bathed in the bright God light, has a life review, and an encounter with angelic beings or the being of light will not necessarily cause maximum life-altering effects either. Having said that, however, I must reaffirm that the majority of the truly psychically gifted people had very profound happenings.

Helen now lives in Vienna, Austria, where she has opened a spiritual healing center. Some of the teachers from Delphi have gone there to give courses, with Helen as the interpreter. I met her at Delphi. Her initial experience was actually "short," but it set her on a path in search of universal knowledge and allowed her to be open to other spiritually transforming events. Her intuitive abilities began increasing immediately after the NDE.

In 1966, when I was seventeen years old, I was put to sleep in the operating room for an appendectomy. The next recollection I have, I was running and it seemed to gain momentum from a slow jog to a *vruuuum*. Actually, I was already in a tunnel, which was lighted. It was very long, almost never-ending. There was a very, very bright light and I had the feeling that I had to go there. I had the feeling that the light was peace, joy, freedom, and lightness, and that is what pulled me forward. The tunnel looked like a swirl. It wasn't black, but the inner part of the tunnel was darker. At the end it looked like an eclipse, made of translucent light, with rays around it. So the tunnel was sort of like the swirls in a seashell cone. The more I felt that I had to go there, the more I could feel my body running and running, and actually my legs were hurting! The closer I got to the other end, the stronger was the feeling of peace, caring, softness, and no worries or burdens, like something heavy was leaving me. I have to tell you that while I was running I felt like I had to do this alone. I was alone my whole life. I felt if I'd get there, then all the loneliness and the feeling of rejection and not being wanted would go away. I knew that the light was no stranger to me. I looked over my shoulder, back at my body, thinking that I had to get away from that. Then, all of a sudden, whammo, I felt my cheek burning and I knew the nurse had hit me. The moment I woke up I vomited, and it hurt so badly right in my solar plexus. I heard the recovery room nurse say: "Oh, God, look at the mess she made, now we'll have to change everything!" I thought to myself: "Ha, ha, that's what you get for getting me back here." I was very angry I was back. This is years and years after, now, and it's still very clear.

I asked Helen how the experience impacted on her religious beliefs. She said:

The Church and its teaching is not true. There is no heaven and hell over there. Hell is over here. In Austria everyone dresses in black for funerals and kneels at a grave praying to a stone. God is all-loving and all-knowing and omnipotent, yet they tell you you're bad, rotten, and will go to hell. The knowing that there is something that gives you ultimate peace, joy, and love is what is important.

I asked Helen what she felt was the bottom line. Her answer:

This experience is an imprint, and it will never go away. We are multidimensional. We are energy beings. We are astral beings. People that have had these experiences should read so they will understand the meaning of what they went through. After I read, I got that "ah-hah" feeling, like "gee, it was so simple!" The knowledge of our energy system, of our etherical, mental, and astral bodies was put away for a long time. Now more and more people understand what energy is. Energy is constant change, constant movement. The understanding of this experience will open doors.

These experiences are so profound that it's almost like an awakening, where someone will ask: "What happened to me?"and then they begin questioning. There ought to be books like [those] by Kübler-Ross in hospitals and clinics so patients can read them. Doctors and nurses should read them to begin with, to understand spirituality. In Austria, there is still a death room in hospitals. If they know you're a goner, then they leave you in there. The person who goes into the death room knows he is dying, even though no one has told him, and he is scared to death. Everyone comes in crying. This is terrible. But if these people understand that our consciousness goes on after death, then there should be less fear. Death itself will die when we all know that we always live. There is no need for death. It's like a programming. It's what you think will happen. People don't want death, so just think of life! The word death should be eliminated. There should only be changes in life, transformations, so that death is really just another adventure of life.

Sadhana is also a truly gifted "psychic." Her heritage is Native American. Her NDE occurred when she was studying in India. She now lives in Taiwan for part of the year, and in Sedona, Arizona for the rest of the year. I met her at Delphi. She related her story:

> I know better than to drink water from the tap in India, but this day I touched the lip of the cup with my mouth. I didn't drink, but perhaps my lips touched the water as a gesture, because I was a guest in someone's home. They had very kindly provided me with cool water in the heat of the tropics. In less than an hour I was feeling very, very ill. I went to my house. This progressed so rapidly that perhaps within two hours I was tossing and turning with fever. I wasn't really conscious. I was laying down on the bed which happened to have been made up with pink sheets, tossing and turning, hair matting in the water of the sweat.
>
> The first thing was I saw myself sitting at the bottom of the bed, cross-legged as we tend to do in India, and also saw the body that was tossing and turning there. But the body was laying on green sheets! The body that was watching the body which was tossing and turning and unconscious, knew it would be well because green is the color of healing. The one that was watching was totally relaxed and there was a total consciousness. I will explain to you.
>
> What I am saying is that the first body is called the watcher and the second is called the witness, and is not cognitive and does not communicate with the other and as you well know, we get into difficulty using language talking about these things. The "I" that was at the bottom of the bed felt a presence at my left shoulder, which I knew from training in meditation was the witness. Sometimes shamans speak of death standing at your left shoulder. I was immediately drawn into the witness, which has no thought, but had total awareness, but does not cognate, doesn't understand. It's merely a witness.
>
> From there I moved swiftly, because I knew to go for the light. Don't bother with anything else, since everything else is finished. Just go for it! So I shot for the light. As you rise,

everything is so exquisite that you want to stay there. You can just think anything and it happens! Colors and sounds are much, much more beautiful than anything that you can at all imagine on this side, both variety and exquisiteness. I understand that this is a plane where many artists and musicians get their inspiration. I'm sure that many would like to stay there after crossing over, because it is so exquisite.

But one must concentrate and stay with going into the light. You keep going through the light and you will go beyond and beyond and beyond. You will go beyond time and eventually you will go beyond space. There is no space at some point. You will also go beyond having any body whatsoever, and after that you will have only awareness. Dropping the body gives such a freedom of not being confined! You're never perfectly well, but you don't know that until you don't have a body. As you rise further, you come into such bliss, not joy, but I mean bliss. Then you go further, beyond even experiencing, and you find it is a freedom to have no emotions, no experiences. If you keep going to the light, and I hate to use the word "I" again, but I went all the way to the Godhead. Boy, that's not even the right words, but anyway, I went to the place where I no longer exist as a separate entity. It's like a drop in the ocean. You are totally dissolved. There is no separate consciousness. There is a vastness, and you are dissolved in whatever words we use for the Godhead.

When you come back, you know that there was no separation. All there is, is all there is. I have no idea how much earth time elapsed during the experience, but as I came back (by now in a hospital), I noticed there was total awareness and total clarity. The first thought I had was that I must remember the way back so I can show others the way.

———

Kacie is one of the subjects who "woke up" with her "toe tagged" in a hospital morgue. She was in her twenties at the time. When she was a child, she had an invisible playmate whom she now feels was a spiritual guide. Her psychic abilities have increased substantially since her Near-Death Experience. The illnesses leading up to her apparent death were presumed aplastic anemia (meaning that the bone marrow stopped producing blood products) and kidney disease. She came back healed of both problems. She stated:

> I just got very sick one day with bad back pain. I couldn't even get out of bed. It was like when an Indian says: "I'm going to die now," goes and sits under a tree, and dies. I kept getting sicker and sicker and was seeing the doctor every day. All of a sudden I got to where I couldn't keep anything down and had to be admitted. My hematocrit was 19 and dropped to 17 right away. They were asking me to line up friends who could donate blood for me. However, I died in the meantime.
>
> Weirdly, my blood cell count and my kidneys were absolutely normal when I came back. Of course, the doctor will say to you that he can't understand how I could have died because if I went that long without my brain getting oxygen then I would be a vegetable. So he says that he really thinks I was alive but they just misdiagnosed me as dead. But remember, they're the ones who put me in the morgue. When I woke up in there I was freezing, so I got up, got off the table and I opened up the door. I was looking down the hall because I was freezing, and I was naked, and I didn't even have a towel to wrap around me. So I finally saw this nurse. She sees me and of course starts screaming and goes running down the hall to pick up a phone. Then these doctors came in there and eventually they gave me back my room. I told them I wanted to talk to somebody about what happened to me, but I guess they were afraid I would sue them. I knew everything would be fine because of the experience. I'll tell you what happened when I died.
>
> I had closed my eyes, was laying in the hospital bed, and I just kinda' sorta' floated out. It wasn't like I got yanked out of my body, but my coming out was almost like a peeling effect. My spiritual body felt like it was coming out of my physical body. It felt like going through a doorway, like a breeze or

something. But I also knew I was pure energy at that point. I wondered if anyone could see me or, if there was a little child there, if the little child could see me and the adults couldn't. Then all of a sudden it was like a vacuum cleaner. I kind of got sucked up, and I was moving real fast through space. All of my body was behind me, so I didn't see any of my body. The freedom that I felt was completely peaceful, and there was this light in front of me. It was like the light of the sun. It was white, but it had kind of yellowish tinges in it and blue.

I had the sense of being a free life force. I had complete freedom, and anything I wanted I could create by just thinking about it! In other words, if I thought "go faster," then I went faster. If I thought "slow down," then I could've slowed down. It only takes a thought to create something. On my way to the light I had the sense of peacefulness and calmness and, I don't know how to say this, but I would say pure love. But I think it even goes beyond that. It's just that everything is perfect. Everything is right. Nothing else matters. It's just that you're bathed in it, almost like you're the pure feeling itself. It's almost like you become one with the feeling, if you could ever feel yourself becoming one with an emotion. It's like, wow! Now I know where I belong, that type of thing. I belong right here.

And then there were these beings that I could sense, with the refraction of light around them. It wasn't like there was a concrete idea of the shape of their bodies, but it seemed like their bodies were taller and, like, their arms were longer and thinner, and their shoulders were narrower, but you didn't know for sure. You couldn't see a hard edge around the body. It was not like a pure silhouette, though.

When I was going toward the light I kind of slowed down because I felt there was something I might run into, only because I saw the flickering in the light. As I got closer I saw there were shapes taking form, but it was like three spiritual beings refracting the light behind them. I actually heard this voice, that I thought was the voice of an uncle who is dead, saying: "You can't come any further." I said: "What do you mean I can't come? I can do anything I want, can't I?" And he said: "Well, yes, but you need to go back. You're not finished yet. You have to go back. Now is not the time." I felt like, pardon the pun, that we were getting into a "spirited discussion." Then, all of a sudden, there was this other being, and I got the impression that it kind of, like, had more seniority. He was like a more powerful kind of person, and I can see where some people might think, if they saw this being, that they were in the presence of Jesus Christ. I could also see how someone might think it was Moses. Now, about the one that was playing my uncle, was it really the spirit of my uncle or was it someone who wanted to communicate with me and was using that familiar person as a translating thing? I don't care! The point isn't who said it, but what was said, or that an intellectual exchange took place.

This other being came from behind, and then was standing in front. I sensed it was a he more than a she, because there was a strong sense of authority behind the spirit or entity. It wasn't something that was evil. It wasn't something that was like God, okay? Although, I see why people could believe that it was God. I believe that God, being a spiritual being, could be very much like this person, just the same as Jesus Christ or Moses, or even Martin Luther King, for that matter. It was immaterial. He didn't speak much, but just said: "You are welcome here, but your time is later." It was almost like I was in a submarine at this point. I was close to the doorway, like being in a long narrow room looking out. I've heard people say tunnel, but this wasn't like that. What difference does it make?

I was just suddenly there. When you are here on this planet, you're stuck here on this planet. You're stuck in your body. It's easy to think about the past, to think about the future, and to get them all mixed up with the present. But over there, you only have the present. You don't have the past and you don't have the future, because none of that is important. Only that moment is important. And it isn't like a rule that someone gave you when you were taught that this is how you're gonna' think. It's kind of a natural thing.

When we were looking over my life I didn't have, like, a tribunal. There was this one big spirit, like the Big Master, as I call him. He kind of took his arm, or what would be the image of a long skinny shadow with a little bigger lump on the end, and was gesturing me over to the side of this submarine. There was a big porthole window that, all of a sudden, was in front of my face. He was encouraging me to look through it, almost like when you watch Scrooge at Christmas and the ghost of Christmas past doesn't say anything, but just points. I knew what he was doing.

It was like he was saying: "I know you need a reason to go back, so look at this." That was the feeling, a loving feeling. So I go look through this porthole, and as I get closer everything starts coming into focus. I saw my boyfriend at the time in bed with a new girlfriend of mine in Fort Myers. I turned to the spiritual being and I said: "You see what I'm talking about? I don't want to go back." And he kind of implied: "If you wish to stay then you can stay, and if you wish to go back then you can go back. But let us show you something else." Then he showed me this other window. I looked into it. I was looking at a far-away image, and it's like you're zooming in on it. So I go down and I feel this "whooosh" sensation where I kind of, like in the movie *Ghost*, suddenly was in this body. But this wasn't my body. I looked down at my hands, because now I had arms, and I had a pen in my hand and a piece of paper in front of me and a bottle of pills. I was writing this suicide letter. But it wasn't me. It wasn't my letter. It was my girlfriend who used to live down here, but has since moved to Orlando. We've had many conversations about suicide, the philosophical aspects. She'd said that nothing could ever be so bad that one would be reduced to taking their own life. But here I was in her body, feeling her pain. I was holding her pen and reading the letter she had written, through her tears, tasting the saltiness of those tears that were dripping down my face into my mouth. All of a sudden, whoooosh, and I was right back there in the submarine.

The spirit said: "So are you ready to go back now?" and I said: "I understand her pain, but it's not enough reason for me to go back and deal with this crap." Then he showed me another window. It was like there was a discussion going on, and I was like eavesdropping on the conversation in some corporation or business somewhere. By the things they were saying I realized they were talking graphic arts and about some person doing a nationwide newsletter. I realized it had to have been me that they were talking about. I said: "Do you think this is a good reason to go back, so people can talk about me behind my back and say wonderful things? I don't want to do a newsletter. This isn't my idea of happiness." The spiritual being said that they wouldn't force me.

Then here comes this spiritual guide into the picture. You have to imagine this old grandfather-type character, very gentle, very old, very wise. It was like I was a child of the universe wanting all the answers now, and this spiritual being was saying: "You have plenty of time." He was telling me to have faith, that I didn't need money and should trust in the profits of life. He was laughing at me, but kindly, like I was some stubborn little kid. Anyway, he showed me another porthole. When I looked, it was another room with people talking about reading about me in the papers. Either I'm supposed to invent something or do something with children. Back in the submarine the spiritual guide said: "Nothing is as important as you going back and leading the children. They're all waiting for you. People will come to you to help make it happen and you need to be there when they come. Everything is going to be fine."

Then he showed me one more window. In it there was this extremely old woman, over eighty. She had all these children sitting around her. Well, I told him I still didn't want to go back, but then I felt a push, like on my chest. It's kind of like when you're trying to go up an escalator and it's going the wrong way. I felt like my intent to move forward was not succeeding. I was losing the battle and I was really moving backwards, closer back to the body that I didn't want. It seemed like I went backwards for three days at a speed faster than light. Then, bam, I opened my eyes and I was in the morgue of the hospital on a stainless steel table with my toes tied together and my name on a tag. That aggravated me!

Since I came back here I went to work for a company that I was marketing director for. I ended up writing articles that were published in leading trade journal magazines. I was declared one of the four industry experts about certain aspects of the field of pawnshops. So I did end up having a lot to do with graphic arts.

All of this has taught me that if you make a move in the direction you think you're supposed to go, and you're going in the right direction, then doors will open. When you're not going in the right direction, then spiritual guides will close doors around you to get you to look for the open ones to help steer you and nudge you in the right direction. I honestly believe that that's how the universe works.

I still feel a connection to those spirits, at least three that I could pick out of the crowd. If everyone has three, then I can see why some people say there was the trinity, meaning the Father, Son, and Holy Spirit, that met them. I believe heaven is in that light, but I wasn't allowed to get there. The only thing I can't figure out is why they kept telling me I had free will and that I didn't have to come back. But I was thrown back against my will.

As soon as I got back into a regular room with a telephone, I called up that friend. She said she'd had the weirdest experience. She said: "I was sitting here and all of a sudden I sensed you were in the hospital dying. You were drifting away and I couldn't stop you." I told her what happened to me and she admitted that she was writing a suicide note. She said it was like all of a sudden I came to her, touched her hand, and was telling her not to do it. She said there was something so convincing about it that she changed her mind!

I have to tell you that one of the amazing things about all this is that when I came back, the blood problem was okay. It wasn't anything the doctor did. Also, my kidneys stopped failing and the function came back to normal.

How long is eternity? Too long! When I finally get spiritually balanced then I'll get the lesson of patience down. It'll be a lifelong lesson for this lifetime, I can tell you that. And, yes, my psychic abilities are steadily but slowly increasing. I can be walking in Wal-Mart, the only person in the aisle, get halfway down and all of a sudden I'll hear a noise, turn around, and stuff will start falling off the shelf. I do believe that my spirit guides are with me.

I think when we are born, we have all the memories from where we've been, that place between lives or whatever you want to call it. It's the place in the sun. Now don't get me wrong. The way I think it works is that, as a spiritual being, the heat of the sun won't matter to you. You don't feel the heat of the sun if you're pure energy, so what better hiding place for someone who can't feel the heat of the sun? Also, the brightness of the light won't hurt you. What better hiding place to be in on this side of the galaxy? But everyone has his own idea of heaven. Where do you think heaven is? They'll say it's some place beyond. Beyond what?

Kacie is now writing children's books and is also doing fantasy art. She has blessed South Florida IANDS by bringing some of her fabulous art work to show us. It is obvious that her increased psychic abilities are manifesting in her art work. She is also doing psychic readings. I can verify that she quite accurately predicted exact dates of both the conception and birth of several babies. The very interesting fact is that all those mothers were told by the medical profession that they were infertile.

Kacie feels very fortunate that during her Near-Death Experience she was shown future events of this lifetime. It did prove to give her clarity and direction. I must say that some of the information that she has brought through from the other side is astounding. Because of that NDE she learned to follow spirit! Like the quote from an unknown author that I love: "May I never miss a rainbow or a sunset because I am looking down," Kacie is always looking up now!

Ron is of Native American heritage, now in his mid-fifties. Half a century ago he drowned in a body of water that was very important to the Iroquois nation. He remembers it "as if it was seconds ago!" He credits the Near-Death Experience with the outstanding ability that he has to channel healing. He relates the event:

> It helps to briefly understand that I was an only child. Everyone treated me very well, with a lot more respect than most young people, so I always thought of myself as very gifted and able to handle almost anything that would come my way. I didn't think in terms of money, although I am an economist and an engineer. Being spiritual for me was a whole lot different than it might be for other people. My grandmother took care of me up to the time I was four and then she passed on, just after World War II.
>
> I moved from a town with sidewalks, in upstate New York, to the country, the Mohawk Valley. Life became very strange for me. It was all downhill from a kid's point of view.
>
> We had a toboggan. Half a mile from my grandfather's house was a field. We used to walk in a cow lane and over the creek, which was very important from the standpoint of Indian lore. There was a huge hill. On the toboggan first you'd go fifty feet, then all of a sudden pick up speed and go all the way down the hill and across the creek. One day we did it all day long and were getting more and more tired. Remember, I was just a little boy. Around four o'clock, in the winter time, it gets much colder all of a sudden and the runs are much faster. I was a fat little boy in all those winter clothes. It was my toboggan, so I got to sit in front, and the cousins and neighbors were right behind me. We all decided that for the

last run of the day we would try to go all the way across the creek and across the field, so we wouldn't have to walk as far home. We were really pushing it.

We hit the creek and the ice cracked. I went through the ice and under the ice. The water under the ice, that normally would be quite small, was quite rapid, very substantial, with a tremendous current. I was being pushed further and further under the ice and then upside down. I lost my footing and was going further away from the crack that I'd fallen into.

While this was happening I was in the midst of the brightest light you would ever want to see. And there were like multiple barriers. As you go through each of these barriers, the light gets brighter and brighter. It's like a platinum light, creamy. You have no sense of fear at this point. You're not scared anymore. You don't have to worry about anything. Everything was so tranquil, yet I could hear all kinds of background noise which you might refer to as clicking. I know it has to do with the heavenly bodies that are all there, trying to talk at the same time.

The one heavenly body who helped me the most I refer to as the Great Holy Spirit. That entity must have been appalled at how I looked. I bet he'd never seen a papoose that looked like me before. Remember, I was upside down and my head was dragging on the bottom as the current was taking me away. The Great Holy Spirit touched me four times. With the first touch he stopped me from being taken any further by the undercurrent. With that touch I got some memories from him. With the second touch he righted me, turned me over, and I got tremendous information with that touch. I was being touched by pure spirit. I was getting power and memories. The third touch was when he was pushing me against the current back toward the crack in the ice. The fourth touch was when he pushed me, with all my weight and all of my soaked winter clothes, up through the crack in the ice.

This tiny, tiny, skinny, five-year-old girl, a cousin, was the only one who was light enough to walk on the ice to where the crack was, without cracking it further. All the other children pulled on her as she pulled on me. But it really wasn't that tiny little girl that pulled me out. I was being pushed up from below.

That entity is named Otstungo, The Holy Spirit. He had come from some great distance and time. That creek is the most ceremonial of all the Mohawk Indian creeks. It's just a small creek now, but it was talked about last year in National Geographic. One of the feeders for this creek is where all the Indians chiefs in the Iroquois nation were named. So because of all the ceremonies there, it was an extremely spiritual creek. It was a great waterway even up through Revolutionary times. Otstungo, The Holy Spirit, had lost his son in this waterway. He has continued to do battle protecting it, to be sure that no one else will ever lose their life there. Some of the information, including memories, that I got from him when he touched me, was about tribal things. I know about land travel before glacier times. There were runners and travelers. I believe that a great meteor came to this area with crystalline intelligence.

I questioned Ron about his spiritual healing ability. He said:

I always knew after being a boy that I had the ability to help people to heal. I knew it was connected to the Great Holy Spirit. I used to think that if I used the healing too much that I would lose it, so I was real careful how I used it. Now I use it every day in every way. The more I use it the more multiplied I feel I've become. Healing is absolute loving. The entire process of healing is the journey back to Our Father. We do get stronger and stronger as we use our healing abilities. We get more powerful. When I'm doing a healing, it's that special feeling you know. I often see movement in my peripheral vision, about sixty degrees above the person, or I see like a mist and the person becomes iridescent to me.

———————

Jarod, a lawyer, attributes his markedly increasing psychic abilities to the fact that he had not one, but three Near-Death Experiences. All three were secondary to neurologic events which occurred because of atrial fibrillation, an irregularity of the heart rhythm. He sustained a cardiac and respiratory arrest which resulted in a most profound core NDE. He describes the first episode:

The first one happened on May 9, 1983. I was fifty-six. I was in the coronary care unit of a New York City hospital. Many people were dying in that unit. They were able to bring back some. And there I was with heparin in both arms, and I'm not responding. They couldn't get my blood thinned. I have a recollection of ringing the bell and not getting an answer.

I know I had a body separation. I looked down and I said to myself, if you'll forgive the French: "Who is that gorilla?" I looked like a gorilla. Then I recognized myself. I was up near the high ceiling. I floated through the walls and down the corridor above the nurses' station. A board was lit up and a bell was ringing and buzzers were going off. No one noticed me. There was no pain, no anxiety, no fear, just peace and quiet. I looked over my shoulder and I started seeing something develop, you know, out of nothing. It was like how a volcano starts, with a little eruption, but this was much faster. There was a bit of noise, like a rustling.

Then suddenly I found myself floating in darkness, being carried along by a current of some sort, like a boat going down a river. Then the pace started to accelerate. It resembled a very dark wind or railroad tunnel. It was enormous with concentric, circular bands at regular intervals. I reached the end rapidly, and suddenly I was in a sea of bright, slightly golden, white light, like an immense brilliant white fog, but much denser and heavier. It was literally a sea of light, which penetrated my every pore and atom and interacted with every cell. That light envelops you, thoroughly penetrates and soaks your every subatomic particle. You are a part of it and it is a part of you. I knew I had been a part of this light before and was merely returning to my proper place where I belonged. This was home, not the earth down here.

To me the sea of light is God, the Creator. I subsequently had contact with a being of light. I feel the being of light is apparently God's chief of staff, His Major Domo, and perhaps His alter ego or aspect. He is a being different from and far superior to any human being like Moses, Abraham, or Buddha, or any archangel. He has some of the same energy as the sea of light and is unique. He never told me that He was a divine Christ, i.e. God the son, second person of the blessed trinity. I communicated with Him.

All of a sudden I felt this total overwhelming love, total compassion, and perfect understanding. It was emotion increased a millionfold. It is literally indescribable, even using this apparently parabolic language. It was love I had never received on earth because we are all human. I felt I was home. Ecstasy would be a very mild and totally inadequate descriptive word for what I felt.

Once I fused with the light, I didn't have any questions. Almost immediately I began to understand the answers to problems which had puzzled me all my life. I had the impression I tapped into a source of universal knowledge. I literally seemed to understand everything, but most of the answers were wiped from me. But I do have tantalizing tidbits of information and vague recollections, just enough to thoroughly frustrate me.

I had a review of my life in 3D and color. It took place without any framework or staging. Sometimes I was the spectator and sometimes I was part of the action. Two guides placed themselves on either side, flanking me. I was reliving my own life, every emotion, every sound, every sight, every smell, every nuance, people's emotions, my emotions, the people who hurt me and how I felt, the people I hurt and how they felt, even how bystanders felt. It was total recall. I really thought I had screwed up my life badly. I really have so many talents, unused, that I thought I'd wasted my life. My wife has always complained that I'm a good-natured slob, but they thought that was important! I'm an easy mark. They, meaning the guides, thought being an easy mark was important! I did all kinds of things in the war, for patriotism. I'm a decent man, with a lot of intestinal fortitude, but I don't think I could do that again. These guys were empathetic. They were also telepathic. I thought to myself: "Oh, crap!" and these guys started chuckling. I came across some stuff that I was feeling badly about, but they said: "That's not so bad. You had your reasons." It was real forgiveness. They didn't judge me. I judged myself, and I'm apparently tougher on myself. They were trying to bolster me up all the way through this. At the end of the review I came to the conclusion that the most important things in life are decency, love, and helping your fellow man.

The guides took me to a place which I will describe as a universal library. It was a vast enclosed space. Depending on what I thought and where I stood, I could get a stream of information on all sorts of topics. Moving about the library was instantaneous. If I wanted to be in another part, I would suddenly be there. The library had no visible machinery, interior walls, offices, or furniture. There were no visible books or scrolls. The building could change from transparent to translucent.

I saw crystal cities, cities of light. The countryside looked like paradise from afar, but there were smaller gardens of Eden (or Allah) closer by. The flowers seemed to communicate with each other. Sometimes they changed colors a little and moved in unison. I'd say there was intelligence in every bud—flower intelligence. The grass, too, has intelligence. It's technicolor to the nth degree. If you were down here and saw grass rhythmi- cally swaying to the music and changing color you'd think you were hallucinating. And the music surpassed anything I ever heard down here.

I believe the light is my Creator. In the light I was home where I belong. Perfect love, perfect understanding. I feel

myself a part of the universe and of our Creator, and I feel
them as literally a part of me. I never wanted to leave that
state of ecstasy and bliss. I came back reluctantly. I believe the
experience was premeditated, but not by me. I think it was
necessary to increase my spirituality in order to get me ready
for a mission which involves healing and teaching. That's my
purpose. That's why I'm still here.

Jarod was obviously very blessed to have had that profound event.
He has subsequently undergone many life-altering changes. Upon his
return from the other side, he was healed of both the stroke and the
atrial fibrillation. He has truly been on a spiritual quest. He reads
constantly, and has studied with some of the most gifted spiritual
healers in this country. He is presently toying with the idea of writing
a book on comparative healing techniques. Jarod embodies what Sir
Thomas Brown was talking about when he said: "All the wonders you
seek are within yourself."

Eve is another medium whom I met at Delphi. Her Near-Death
Experience occurred in 1976, when she was twenty-six years old. Eve
suffers from sleep apnea, a sleep disorder where breathing ceases for
ten seconds or longer. It is a relatively rare disorder, occurring in
approximately three percent of the population, less common in
females than in males. More is known about sleep apnea now than
when Eve's experience occurred. It may be treated with surgery where
indicated or with a device used during sleep that produces continu-
ous positive airway pressure. Here is her story:

I had a history of stopping breathing during the middle of the
night. Most of the time I would just wake myself up catching
my breath, gasping for air. This particular night I went to bed
early. My kids, eight and four, were asleep. My husband was
out of town. I guess I stopped breathing for a long period of
time. When I woke myself up this time, I was on the floor of

the bedroom, or thought I was, and there was a candle in the window. It was just sitting on the sill of the window, burning. I saw the candle and thought: "This is strange that I would be on the floor in the first place, and second, that there would be a candle in the window." We didn't burn candles, especially at night. There could be a fire!

As I looked at the candle, the glow from the light increased until it covered the whole window. Then the glow got bigger and bigger and bigger until it not only covered the whole window, but it went out and beyond. All of the light seemed to be, from my perspective on the floor, coming from that candle. All of a sudden I realized I wasn't laying on the floor, but that my body was in the bed. So one body was on the bed and one body was on the floor.

The body that was on the floor started to get up to go see the candle. When I got up it was like the light was calling to me. I went through the window, through the drapes, through the glass, through everything in the window. I went into the light and went *with* the light out into wherever it went. It was more than light. It was *holy*! It was as if it went all the way through my body that wasn't my body. It was warm and fuzzy and kind. It was just total pure joy! It was pure comfort. It was everything you could imagine ecstasy being. It was just being. You didn't have to do anything but just agree to be in it. So I *was* in it out there, and I realized that the candle was still burning in the window. I realized the kids were sleeping in their bedrooms and there's no way I could leave the candle burning with them asleep.

I didn't want to come back. I was already out there. I was already gone, and wanted to think that if I went, then the candle would just eventually go out by itself. But I couldn't just go. Then it was the feeling of the most utter sadness, that I had to come back and put that candle out. So I came back through the window, over the candle, to the body on the floor. I kept trying to reach up to put the candle out, but the body on the floor couldn't put it out. It's like I'd touch it and blow on it, but it wouldn't go out.

Then I looked over and there was the body on the bed. So I thought: "This is ridiculous. There's a body on the floor that can't do anything and there's a body on the bed that looks dead and can't do anything!" The only choice I had then was for the body on the floor to get back into the body on the bed, 'cause that's the only way I could get that candle out. So the body on the floor did get up and get back into the body on the bed, but then the body on the bed realized it couldn't breath! So I still couldn't get that candle out. This was awful and seemed to last for hours and hours. So I willed myself to wake up and start breathing. I finally woke up and the candle was gone!! I thought about it for days and months. I never told anyone about it until now.

I asked Eve to tell me about the light. She said:

The vibrancy of that light was like no vibrancy here. It wasn't like fluorescent lights. It was a higher vibration. It was total love. It penetrated me thoroughly. It was funny. As I went through the window and I was on the outside, I was looking back at that body on the bed. It was like I was the reality and the body was the unreality. It was like looking back at an empty stage. That out there was so vibrant and alive and all-encompassing. It was just so total! But what I was seeing looking back through that window was just so empty, like a bare stage. The body laying on the bed was dead. It had no life in it. It wasn't mine anymore. That's why I was so sad that I had to come back to it.

I asked Eve what she would say to someone who was dying, to comfort them. She answered:

I would say that the soul has much to do. This act in the play is only that: an act in the play. The play is so much bigger than we can even imagine. Dying is like fading out of one scene and into another. The hard part, the part we should almost mourn, is the child coming on to this earth, not the child leaving this earth, because leaving this earth is going home. It's going back to spirit. It's going back to love. It's going back to beauty. It's going back to God. Coming into this earth is separating the soul from everything that is beautiful. We have to do this to learn what we have to learn. It's like sending a first-grader to school. When you send him away from his mother, you put him on a school bus and you send him to this enormous school with this crabby first-grade teacher and other kids who are brats that treat him awful. Then he comes home and you ask him: "How was your day? Did you have a good time in school? Did you learn anything today?" Well, he learned that his mother doesn't take care of him now, but sends him off on a bus to a horrible school. So when we come to earth we're taken away from everything warm and wonderful and are put into a schoolroom to learn lessons that we really don't understand until we've learned them. The first-grader doesn't appreciate his high school diploma until the morning after he gets his high school diploma. He doesn't see it in the first grade. Can we see what we have done on this earth now? No! We're like in the fifth grade now.

Eve now applies her intuitive and channeling abilities to counseling others. There is a saying that the greatest good that we can do for others is not just to share our riches with them, but to reveal their own riches to themselves. This summarizes Eve's life's work at this point in time.

Don is an accountant. When he was thirty-six he was a meteorologist in the Air Force, stationed in Honduras. He became severely dehydrated with food poisoning, and knew he didn't have the strength to get to the infirmary, so he went to bed. He said:

I left my body and found myself in darkness. Then I found myself at the feet of Jesus. Everything was white. Jesus had a white robe on. He had light brownish hair. I saw His face. He glowed! He was taller than me, but how tall am I in spirit? He spoke to me. It was a mental thing. He said: "Come in. It's okay." Behind Him I could see like a screening room and I knew I was going to have to revisit my life. I haven't been that bad, but for some reason I just didn't want to face it. I was afraid to face it. In that screening room I saw other men, maybe other spirits, that were reviewing their lives. The room was all white, four walls, and a table. Some of them were sitting at the table. The next thing I know, I'm tumbling over and over, like through a dark tunnel toward my body. It was very quiet, then I suddenly stopped tumbling and was laying on my back with my feet up and I heard this loud roaring noise. I know I was in the space shuttle that exploded, but I hope it was the Columbia that already exploded and not one in the future. It exploded and then I was tumbling back again and tumbled into my body. I hit my body rather hard and even felt the bed shake.

Since his NDE, Don has been blessed to have had several experiences where he has seen angels. When his grandfather died, 2,000 miles away, Don found himself out of his body witnessing the event. Everything Don related was verified by a family member who was bodily there. Don has clairvoyant dreams, which are increasing in frequency and import. He is also able to see auras now. He faithfully attends South Florida IANDS and his presence contributes greatly to our group.

Charles Nunn has had many Near-Death Experiences. His psychic abilities became so magnified, as a result, that he has been a professional in the field of metaphysics for more than eighteen years. He was one of the most outstanding teachers of mediumship and spiritual healing that I had at Delphi. He is a spiritual healer, consultant, and researcher of radionics and psychotronics. He is also a lecturer and teacher of metaphysics and spirituality, a certified hypnotherapist, a

Reiki Master and Teacher, a certified Somatic Healer, and an ordained minister. As an intuitive consultant, Charles advises businesses, institutions, and individuals around the world. I must say that the descriptions of his Near-Death Experiences come very close, for me, to the Holy Grail of NDEs. As Edith Wharton said: "There are two ways of spreading light—to be the candle or the mirror that reflects it." Charles is both the candle and the mirror.

All the events happened between 1961 and 1991. There were actually seven experiences all together, but I will tell you a great deal about three in particular. They were, for the most part, related to severe kidney problems and Crohn's disease (inflammatory disease of the intestines). My life changed considerably every time I had one of those experiences. I've had five kidney operations over the years, and each time I had one it made the Crohn's disease worse.

The first one was in 1961. I had come home from college and, as usually happened, I would wake up in an ambulance or in the emergency room or recovery room. I'd be in the hospital for twenty-eight days at a time. I was a Southern Baptist. I had no explanation for these things, and had not heard the term Near-Death Experience at the time. As far as I was concerned, I was dead.

I was struggling a lot with my Southern Baptist religion, maintaining family businesses and negotiating labor unions and going through strike situations for my family businesses. The stress was incredible. I would get large thumb-sized kidney stones that caused obstruction. That necessitated surgery. Even though I was very stoic, sometimes the pain was very great. I remember that in three different cases I was praying that I would be taken away. I asked Jesus to please just come after me to take me home. Each time I thought I had gone home.

It was not a mental experience, but a feeling experience. I went out through the back of my body. It was like I went out through the top of my shoulders. My feet would drag and

come out where my waist was, but I was in an upward movement when I came out. I came back in the same way. I would
see the nurses and the doctors and the hospital room, and
would then go right through the wall. I had no fear, whatsoever. Then I would find myself on what appeared to be a
white marble or material table, no cloth. I was raised up on it.
It was almost like I was coming up through a floor into a
receptacle that would fit that table, and yet it was nothing that
was solid. It was more vaporous than that. As I was elevated
up, there was what I would have to say was a family of light
beings. This is very difficult to put into words.

They were light beings. Most of them didn't have clear definition, but I could tell the difference between male and
female, although most of them were robed. They had blue
laser-colored eyes and everything about them was silvery platinum. As soon as I would get anywhere near their view, long
beams of blue light would come from their eyes and bathe me
in electric blue. They were blending with me. It wasn't like
they were touching me, it was like they were blending with
me and yet they didn't lose their identification. There was
absolutely no part of me that wasn't loved, touched, and
healed. Crying like a baby doesn't do it justice. It's like tears
would come out of every pore like tears of joy. Their robes
were made of light. They were never vivid enough to see
details, like a cloth robe. They were glowing, shimmering.
They all had long hair. They had arms and legs. I could tell
the robes didn't come all the way down because the arms were
reaching out and touching me and going into my energy. It
wasn't like their hands were touching my body, but it was like
their hands and their energy blended with my body and my
energy. When I would be next to them or when I would
encounter them, I would feel the most exquisite love that I
have ever felt in my life. I've never been able to describe how I
felt, but ecstasy is an understatement.

There was always some sort of music that I am unable to
describe. It didn't seem to be in the background, but it seemed

to be that I was living in the music and I was living in the colors. The first thing I would hear would be tones. I was living in the tone, and then it would become music. It makes me choke up to think about it. It's the most beautiful music I've ever heard. It touched every atom of my being in my physical body, in my aura, in my etheric body, and it was so exhilarating! It was like there were little sparkles going off in every part of it. It was like soaring through the clouds, or more than that, it was like soaring through the oneness. Looking back, I didn't understand this then, but it was like knowing that I was a part of all of it and there was nothing to fear. It's like I was vibrating with the tone and color, and at other times it was like looking through an opaque glass into a physical setting. It wasn't clearly defined, but there were times there were many structures and many other people there. Some of the structures appeared to be white. Some were domed, some had spires, and then there were some that had other geometric shapes. Some were cubed. I'd say they were cities of light.

When I was going up to see the family, the air in that space seemed like it was composed of crystals. It was like the music, solid, yet composed of many parts. The substance of the atmosphere was made out of gillions of crystals. It shimmered in the light. Even my body appeared to be made of gillions of little crystals, and yet there was no cold, hard feeling to them, though it was cool. There was nothing smokey.

It was all very sacred. I didn't encounter one individual more sacred than the rest. I felt a part of it. I wasn't in awe of it, but it was like a natural state of being. Everything was crystalline, moving, and had sound. I was so glad to be there, that there was nothing I needed to ask. It was like everything that had been done or was going to be done was right, in that atmosphere. My body was part of it.

So in the experiences with the family, I was there, unspoken, being refurbished and revitalized and reconnected. Then it was just a natural process to come back. There wasn't a closing of a door, but at some point all of a sudden I'd be jarred, would open my eyes, and be back in the hospital room. I'd look around, and each time I'd be disappointed that I was back, because I realized I was back in the physical body. But each time I looked around, everything looked different. I recognized the place, but in the respect that I've never been able to describe, it looked different. It was like it was a parallel life. It wasn't like the same life I had left.

After each experience I lightened the load of my life. I did quit going to the Baptist church, not because I didn't love it, but just because the realities of what a church and that particular religion stood for no longer had any meaning for me. I found a lot of easier ways to do my work, and wasn't as emotionally involved in it. I withdrew from my marriage after thirteen years. I couldn't explain where I was going, but I knew it wasn't going to continue being corporate life and it wasn't going to be those same social situations that I had grown up in. There was a desire on my part to go back and kind of create the space I had been in and discover the beauty and love and freedom that I felt there. The only way I could do that was to go out west.

You see, each time I had one of those experiences, it was like I finished off an entire lifetime. My response to people and my response to the world situation on a very practical daily level was quite different. Friends noticed that there was a change in my personality and they noticed that I wasn't nearly as nervous. I was able to be healthier every time I had one of those experiences. My reading materials changed. I started reading *Jonathan Livingston Seagull* (Richard Bach, Macmillan, 1970) and it set me on fire, because I knew there was something to life that I had never really been aware of.

I started a construction company. I was doing work for an owner of a restaurant who was Cuban. He took one look at me, then gave me a stack of books including one on the life of Edgar Cayce. When I read that book and it talked about healings, I sat up and thought: "I don't have to take medicines. If you ask for a healing it should happen." After being in all those medical situations all those years, and was supposed to have died, I go so fired up about studying more about metaphysics and healing that I forgot to die! I started taking classes on spiritual matters, have absolutely been healed of my kidney problems and Crohn's disease, and you know the rest.

I asked Charles if all of the experiences were basically the same. He said:

There were two other experiences that I put in the same category of the Near-Deaths, but I wasn't definitely dead. I had moved from Santa Fe to California, married a native Californian, and we bought a ranch on the Oregon border. By then I was just about to become burned-out doing psychic work seven days a week. I was always a workaholic and that didn't change when I worked as an intuitive. I was doing readings for people seven days a week, for a month at a time without a day off. I never advertised. It was all by word of mouth.

As a child I had always wanted to have a horse ranch. So we bought this ranch in the wilderness, surrounded by national forest. I was in a horse accident. The cinch broke and I fell down the mountainside and broke most of my ribs. I had internal injuries. Right in the moment of hitting the ground I went right back into the same space of the Near-Deaths. I saw the loving family with the light bodies and blue laser eyes and had the feeling of ecstasy. Then, instantly, I reexperienced a life in which I had died on the battlefield coming off a horse. I had broken all the ribs and died of those injuries right there on the spot. I was the person experiencing the severe excruciating pain laying on the battlefield in a suit of armor. The squire that was over me at the time, in that past life, turned out to be my wife in this life. She was over me in the same position saying the same things to me and I experienced a total release from the pain for just a few minutes. It seemed to be in France, a big battle, and I'd been knocked off my horse and I lifted right out of my body. I was going into the most beautiful peace and space. I had looked over the battlefield and there were people lying all over. Then I really blacked out, in this lifetime, and finally the medivac helicopter came. They thought I was gone, but I came back.

I asked Charles if he had ever had a life review of this present life. He said:

In one of the early experiences I went back into my childhood. I remembered being alone and choosing to be alone. I was very sickly. I created my own world.

I asked if he received any insights into absolute morality, i.e. what is right and wrong in the absolute sense. His answer:

The tight morality that I had as a Southern Baptist no longer exists. There is a feeling I have that almost everything is appropriate for somebody at some time. We are all here to experience. The rules and regulations are our attempt to try to control our experiences. When we're willing to be more spontaneous and to trust the part of us that knows what we're here for, then morality will look quite different.

I next asked Charles what matters most in life. He replied:

I guess I had to be stubborn to have that many experiences. Either that, or I was slow. All the things I thought were so important, like responsibility, doing the right things, and dressing the right way, just all evaporated. Yet it took a long time to get to the place where I'm comfortable. I know I am here. I know I am spiritual, that we are all one, and that we are choosing to play different roles. In this particular experience I choose to have a good time and to enjoy it.

Love is what it is all about. When I look back at it, the crystals I saw were composing my body and everything in the experience. The crystals are love and contain all the information. That is my priority, unconditional love, experiencing it and living it. That's my daily prayer and my affirmation. Whatever gets in the way of that, or whatever is not of that, I have asked that my attention be brought to it so I can do something about it. So I've had some abrupt awakenings along the way.

With reference to new information about future events, he said:

Yes, I got a lot of information about earth changes and extraterrestrials and how we are all connected. All the old forms are being broken and the only thing that is important is love and unity and cooperation.

I questioned Charles about new goals that he may have. He said: "I want to experience unconditional love in physical form. We all can become one." I also asked Charles what he would say to someone who was afraid to die, to comfort them. He answered:

First I would tell them how much I loved them, and I would mean it. I would hold their hand and allow that feeling to move through them, because at that moment I can feel the same energy that I experienced those times. Having been in that situation myself, I know that a dying person is so sensitive to the situations in the room and to the energy, that I know I don't have to say much. I could be there and be with them, and it's like a smile all over your body. I wouldn't have to say much to them audibly, but I would communicate to them what they are about to experience. It is very beautiful, and the loved ones that they have known in this lifetime and from other times are standing by. Not to worry that they are seeing them. They're here to welcome you. I love you and support you in whatever you want to do. If you want to go back and forth with your friends and loved ones on that side, then feel free to do it. I'll watch the space while you're gone, and make sure nobody bothers you, like medical people trying to save them or relatives clutching at them.

The bottom line?

We're spirit now, but have a physical body. We're spirit then, but have an astral body. We simultaneously exist in all these dimensions. We have a physical body, but when we withdraw from the physical form, we leave a print in the astral that has its own life, too, that evolves also. It's like we rebirth ourselves many times. There are many of us.

I must reiterate that a large percentage of experiencers have a change in their values and beliefs after their NDE. How they live their lives from day to day, therefore, changes.

Also, whether or not the experience was caused by illness, accident, was self-inflicted, or was a result of various other causes, most people begin taking better care of themselves once they integrate what happened into their lives. I don't mean to imply that they all become Herculean specimens, but they do often make very beneficial changes in lifestyle to ensure that their physical container will last longer.

Terry Gilder attends our South Florida IANDS meetings regularly. He is my medical patient. This interview was actually done in the intensive care unit. He had called me that Saturday morning, saying that he had a headache that wouldn't go away and would like an appointment for the coming Monday morning. I was able to convince him to meet me in the emergency room. He had actually ruptured a cerebral aneurysm (a blood vessel broke in his brain). I did the interview as we were waiting for his surgery to be done. Needless to say, he did fabulously well and had a full recovery. He described the Near-Death Experience that had occurred several years before:

It happened when I had a cardiac arrest during surgery for morbid obesity. I weighed over 400 pounds and I was dying. My kidneys were failing, my feet were swollen, I had already had congestive heart failure, and my circulation was bad. I looked like this big egg walking down the street. I went in the hospital after having the psychological testing and the full workup to make sure I was a good candidate. So I was on the operating table, with the intravenous fluids going in. The surgeon said to me: "I'll see you in a little while." I looked at him and said: "I'll catch you later." We both chuckled and that was it.

The next thing I realized, I was above looking down on the operating room, watching what the doctors and nurses are doing. I died. I saw them giving me the electric paddles. When I was watching that, it was like watching a movie with no sound. It was like out of synch. I wasn't afraid. I didn't feel dismay, elation, or anything. It was like a blank page. That big, fat, ugly thing down there wasn't me. The person that was up there was me. So up there, I was out of my shell the way I was supposed to be, looking down at something that wasn't me.

Up behind me, way off to my left, was a light. It was like a hallway. There was a shadowy spot and then a light down there. As I got closer, it was a burst of light, with like finger points all the way around it. I wanted to go there. I felt at ease. I was tired of being fat. I knew there was peace there. I just knew.

You've got to understand that I was a fat person for a long time. I found out what it was like to be discriminated against. It's not a nice thing. I'll tell you a little story. My wife is a lovable person. She loves everybody. But if she had met me when I weighed 474 pounds, she wouldn't have given me the time of day. That's the type of discrimination I'm talking about. You have people who work in the general public that are fat. They are wonderful, intelligent people, but because they're obese their employers stick them in the back where other people can't see them. It goes on all the time. Just for fun, go to stores and check out where the fat people are working. Go to lawyer's offices, real estate offices, a thousand different places, and check out where the fat people are. They're never in front with the public. So I knew what it was like and I knew that there was peace on the other side. It would be peace for me.

I went through another dimension. I didn't have any more cares, no more needs, no more worries, no requirements. I felt totally, absolutely, completely free! But just as I started walking toward that light it was like somebody ran a movie past me. It was my life! And I'll tell you something. There was no cutting out the good parts or cutting out the bad parts. I saw everything: all the good things I'd done, all the horrible things I'd done, even the things I was ashamed of and didn't want people to know. You see it all.

It was like film clips. I saw myself at three, on the playground at an Ottawa park. They [some children] stole my little red wagon. I saw myself walking down the street with my grandmother, telling her it was stolen. She made my grandfather buy me another one, and they stole it again. I saw myself taking a ride with my grandfather in his Hudson Hornet convertible. I lived each piece of the life review. I was in each piece. It's not like watching a movie. It was really traumatic to me. I lived a part where I was sixteen and my parents went away to Detroit and left me to celebrate my birthday party all by myself. I saw when I was twenty-two and married, and a whole bunch of stuff. You know how you make up a picture collage? Well, in my mind this was a collage of my lifetime. I saw when I was eighteen or nineteen and it was Christmas. My mother bought my sister and brother a little present, but said to me: "Honey, we couldn't afford to buy you anything." It hurts! No matter what, it hurts! I try to live my life without hurting anyone.

So it all hangs out in the life review, Kid. There's nothing missing. When I grew up as a Catholic, you were told that God will judge you. That isn't true. You are your judge. You are the hardest, most unsympathetic judge there is when you judge yourself. I guess I'm not ready to go because I haven't learned enough yet. I didn't want to come back, but for some reason I looked back and saw my wife and kids and knew I had to.

I asked Terry how he feels about organized religion since the experience. He said:

I'm a very religious person, but I don't believe in the Catholic church. I believe in God. I've always been against organized religion, but after the NDE happened I was even more so. If a person tried to live good all of his life and he still gets to go where he thinks he's going to, then you don't need organized religion. I've seen too many people starving to death in religious countries. I've seen the abuse and the atrocities that go on by organized religion in the name of God, and they're killing and murdering people by the thousands. Go to any country where organized religion controls. Their education is down, their lifestyle is down, and the standard of living is down. Everything is down, because the Church controls. That's the way I feel. I went to a Catholic Church, regularly, many years ago when we lived in Canada. They were going to excommunicate me because I walked down the street holding hands with my wife-to-be and I kissed her goodnight. Any kind of church that has that kind of power over people doesn't deserve to be a church. A church is supposed to be for the good of the people, to hold people together. It's not supposed to terrorize them, that if they don't live the way the Church says then they're going to bang you to hell. That was the end of the Church for me.

I asked Terry if he feels that he has changed how he lives his life. He answered:

I don't look at life the same anymore. I don't get mad like I used to. I used to have a very, very vicious temper. You, as a doctor, will understand what I'm going to say. Life is like a membrane. It's so fragile that if you're not careful you will step through the membrane and it's over. That's how fragile life is. People don't appreciate how valuable and how fragile our lives are and they abuse themselves and abuse themselves, thinking that their bodies are immortal. They're not. They're there as a wisp.

My biggest problem is that I don't know what my purpose is for still being here. Five times I've been dead and five times

He's sent me back. I was electrocuted twice (I was a master electrician), and hit by lightning twice, and then died on the operating table, like I just told you.

Terry's story has been featured in both a newspaper article and a local magazine article after two journalists attended an IANDS meeting where he shared his experience. Everyone who meets Terry and hears him speak is very moved by his honesty, sincerity, and spirituality. Surely there can be no doubt that his ability to share so genuinely from the heart is one of, if not the, purpose for which he is here. He has been a blessing in my life, as he has been to everyone who has met him.

NINE

Additional Life-Altering Changes

N̸DE and LTP experiencers frequently make life-altering changes, especially in their occupations. The experience leaves them with an increased veneration of life, expanded insights into absolute morality, decreased prejudice, and a belief in free will. They learn the lesson of forgiveness, and commonly affirm to never judge others. They may also find they have trouble with their watches and appliances

Your vision will become clear only when you can look into your heart. Who looks outside, dreams, who looks inside awakes.

—Carl Jung

Additional Common Life-Altering Changes

We must remember that many of these life-altering changes cannot occur at warp speed. They take time to evolve. It is very individualized—everyone does not undergo all, or even most, of these outstanding changes. However, nearly everyone does come back from the other side affirming that the main reason we are here is to learn and to practice unconditional love for our fellow human beings. Most learn to accept people the way they are, and adapt a "live and let live" philosophy. Nearly every subject has an increased veneration of life, knows that one must never never judge another, and learns the divine art of forgiveness.

A change in occupation is common. On many occasions the experience had such profound effects on the person that he or she was no longer satisfied with a job that held no meaning other than the pay check. Experiencers will say that their job now must allow them to grow and truly make a difference in others' lives. If they feel their job does not afford them the opportunity to share what they have learned, then if they don't change jobs, at least they will do volunteer work to help others in a meaningful way. This often involves working with the terminally ill.

Sarah is now a hospice nurse. She was in her twenties, in college, when her Near-Death Experience occurred.

> In 1979 I was whitewater rafting. I got caught in an undertow, my life jacket floated down the river, and I was sucked under water. I was fighting and fighting. I could see the sun above, but I couldn't get to it. I couldn't get out because I was stuck in these rocks. It was one of those high water days. I remember thinking: "I'm gonna' die." Then I got so tired that I thought: "This is it. I AM going to die," and I stopped fighting. Everything turned black. Then it became the most gorgeous, peaceful, wonderful thing I have ever experienced. I saw the tunnel, the light, and figures. I think the light was a higher being, like God. It was definitely a thing more powerful than the sun. I don't think anyone was in the tunnel with me. They were all at the outer edges of it. Have you ever sailed? Have you ever been like ten miles outside of a city on a very dark, gorgeous night? Do you know how velvet it looks?

The tunnel was like that. It was quiet and had that quality of expanse and peacefulness. I could almost touch it. Black velvet would be the best way I can describe it. I was proceeding forward, floating, a very smooth process.

Right in the beginning there were these very quick scenes from my childhood, just little pictures. Like I would see me in a certain dress and remember that day. There were about a half-dozen quick little pictures. I don't know what significance they had. There were people at the other end of the tunnel and that beautiful light was at the other end, too. My grandmother, who had died eons ago, like in the sixties, was there. My father was probably the freshest, because he died within that year. I can remember a couple of aunts and uncles on my father's side, and there were other people that I didn't recognize. They were like ghosts, I guess, because they were in front of the light. It wasn't like they had physical bodies, but they had the shape of a body. I guess it was more their voices that I recognized.

They said that if I wanted to, that I could join them. I said: "No, I'm not ready." They didn't like entice me or anything. I could tell by their demeanor that they were happy where they were. There was no strain involved. I didn't see their mouths move or hear their voices, per se. It was telepathic.

So I consciously chose to come back. Then I don't remember anything for a while. Then I was gasping for air and they pulled me out. They said it was about twenty minutes. This was an Indian reservation, so I had to get back in the raft and finish the day. It was long before cell phones.

It was so incredibly peaceful. There aren't any words to describe it. It was beautiful, magnificent. I remember it as vividly as when I was going through it.

It was years before I mentioned it to anybody. I thought they'd lock me up in a loony bin. I never even told my fiancée. Now I have spoken about it with other hospice nurses at work. You know, as hospices nurses, we have to talk about death with our patients. What I tell them is that I know it is so beautiful and peaceful, that it will be beyond their expectations. When the people are open enough, it's really neat. The families appreciate it, too.

I asked Sarah if she feels she has been changed because of her experience, and what new insights she came away with. She said:

I think it caused me to begin to change and to become more of a spiritual person. The physical wasn't as important as before. I can't say there was a drastic change immediately, but it started me on a path. Now, of course with hindsight, I realized it *was* the turning point. I still wonder why I came back, because it was just so nice and wonderful there. I tell my hospice patients: "You'll see the face of God long before the rest of us. It'll be worth it!"

When I asked Sarah if she has any fear of death, she answered:

I fear the physical pain like everyone else. But since my Near-Death [experience] I pray that I am conscious when I die. I very much hope that I am conscious. That's not how most of the terminally ill hospice patients feel, because a lot of them want to be unconscious at the end and don't want to know.

Sarah wrote to me last December (1998) to say that she has left hospice work, and is now pursuing a practice in Healing Touch. She is working with the energies, redirecting them to flow freely, thus relieving pain and speeding the healing process. I certainly agree that it is a successful adjunct to medical care, emphasizing the "wholeness" of the patient.

———————

Carol is another hospice nurse, now in her fifties. When she had her NDE she was already a nurse, but decided later to do hospice nursing because of the experience.

She had a cardiac and respiratory arrest, and was clinically dead, during her third delivery. She was in her thirties at the time. She states:

I was dead for three minutes. I traveled out of my body. My spirit just flew up and I was above my body and a little to the side. There was a flat green line across the monitor. I saw that, and then I saw the nurses putting the electrical leads on my chest to revive me. One of the nurses was saying: "Oh my God, he's lost her! He's lost her!" The doctor was screaming: "It was just routine! How did we lose her?" So I was watching them work on my body. I wasn't afraid. I had no fear.

I felt very serene, very calm, very relaxed. I felt very nice. Then, next, I was in this tunnel. It wasn't a dark, dingy, scary tunnel. It got lighter and lighter. I was going higher and higher toward this very, very bright light. The light was blue and white. I think there were spirits with me. I didn't feel like I was alone. I felt I was being guided.

Then I saw a very faint face, like a male face. I heard myself saying to him: "I want to go with you. He'll watch the girls." (I was referring to my husband.) The voice said back to me: "He will *not* watch the girls. You'll watch the girls. It is not your time." Then I woke up and I was back on the table. P.S., my husband left me and I did end up raising the girls.

I asked Carol about the consequences of the NDE for her. She answered:

I think one must have an inner peace, a clarity in life. It touches everything and nothing can trade that off. I have that blessing of an inner peace. I feel I don't play the games that other people play. I size people up more carefully than I did before. Material things don't mean anything. I listen to my children more carefully and try to make them understand how important education is. I try to guide them. Also, I know to go only by my gut feeling, or intuition, or whatever you want to call it. I stay far away from negative people and negative energy. Life is too precious. Negativity squeezes out your juice. I feel wonderful that I was one of the ones that was chosen to have that experience.

Tommy is a nurse. I have had the great pleasure of working with him. He had a fascinating experience where he received knowledge in a huge library on the other side. He obviously thirsts for knowledge. I never knew, until we did the interview, that he raises birds. He describes part of his experience:

> The people there looked like they were from Greek and Roman times, dressed in robes or togas, sitting on the grass, which was jade green. The library was a building sort of like the Acropolis, that style. So I went in. There was a whole section of books on palmistry and astrology. I went over to dive into those, but someone told me I wasn't allowed to read those but pointed to some others I could touch. I've always loved birds, so I looked for that section and found it. I took this huge book and saw not only every species of birds that ever was, but every species of birds that will ever be!
>
> Then I went to the section on people. I got to look at my book. I'll never forget it. You opened it up, like in the middle. If you flipped back, you got the past and if you flipped ahead then you got the future. But most of it had this grayish film, so you couldn't read it. Then I could see the day I was born, and grayed over was the day I would die. The impression I got was that I either have to repeat a lesson (because it was grayed over) or I didn't learn it properly so I'll have to repeat what that incident was. I consciously knew that.

Tommy definitely has the ability to act as a channel of healing. This is not self-professed. I have witnessed his abilities. He is very humble, the sort of man William Wordsworth wrote of: "The best portion of a good man's life is his little, nameless, unremembered acts of kindness and of love."

———————

Brenda, an ovarian cancer survivor, described her experience in chapter seven. She changed her occupation after the event. She said:

I stopped managing a brokerage firm that I was part owner of, because I thought the stress probably sped up the cancer. Everything changed for me, especially my relationships with people and with my family. My family saw me differently. They learned to trust that I knew what was best for me, including a more meaningful and less stressful job. You see life so differently after dying. Things that were so important, like money, are really insignificant. You see people differently. When you're living with cancer there's a period you go through where you have to complete everything. But after that experience I find that I'm beginning meaningful things, too.

Trouble with watches, appliances and electrical circuits, in general, is a pretty common occurrence. Melvin Morse, in *Transformed by the Light*, stated: "The idea that the Near-Death Experience changes a person's electromagnetic force field greatly clarifies a number of the changes that take place in NDErs. Spontaneous healings, personality transformation, telepathy, and out-of-body experiences are all paranormal experiences that become normal when viewed in this context."

Morris related his story in chapter six. When I asked him if he encountered any unusual difficulties with electrical or battery operated items, he answered:

I damage a lot of electrical stuff. My TV can turn purple, green, and blue from a change in the electrical field. I've been hit a number of times with electricity. It's God's say of making me pay attention. When I don't pay attention, then He wakes me up.

I have to tell you what happened with this sign wave machine. I would grab the test lead and the screen would go berserk with eight different waves on it. Everybody else would touch it and only get a single, very slow, flow wave across it. Every time I grabbed it, eight different waves went across it. After that everything started to accelerate from there, including my clairvoyant abilities.

Kathi's story was related in chapter one (p. 1). She also said:

> If I get too little sleep for a few days in a row, then my electri-
> cal energies must get out of whack. I've been known to blow
> the transformer out totally, like three or four times. Of course
> the electrical company wouldn't be happy to know it's me. I
> don't do it intentionally. I went to see a girlfriend in Shreve-
> port a couple of years ago. I'd been up for a couple of days get-
> ting ready for the trip. After I got there, I couldn't sleep. I was
> like wired for sound, nervous energy. I blew out the trans-
> former on her block. Since then I've really tried to be more in
> balance with the rest of the world, electrically, anyway. In
> 1980 I bought my first computer and took a class. Well, I
> blew out the motherboard in the computer!

Alexis has been a close friend of mine for many years. Over ten years
ago we traveled to the Orient together. When we were in Seoul,
Korea, we went on a shopping spree. While we were there, I bought
many watches that were copies of famous designer watches. Alexis
didn't buy any, saying simply that she didn't wear a watch. Since this
was prior to beginning my Near-Death Experience research, I never
pressed her for the reason why. When I thought about it, years later, I
called to ask her about it. It was then that I found out that she had an
NDE as a child. It profoundly changed her!! She feels that the occupations she has chosen were also directly related to her experience.

> It happened when I was ten years old, which was thirty-eight
> years ago. I was playing baseball. I was catching, and a boy
> was up at bat. He flung to hit the ball and missed. The ball
> hit me on the head, right on the bone by my left eye. I felt my
> whole body quivering, like a vibration, like energy was com-
> ing out. And I heard a ringing sound. I could hear my father
> shouting, then everything went black. Then there were flashes
> of light and I could hear my father saying: "Oh my God,

you've killed her!" I remember thinking: "So this is what it's like to be dead!" The next thing I knew, I was in the car, but I was on the roof looking down at my body. I felt like a beckoning to go outside the car, and I did. I was floating and had such a feeling of peace! It was almost like a fog or mist. I was going somewhere. I remember thinking of my grandfather, and suddenly I was where he was, watching him. I woke up in pain from the stitches in my head.

I asked Alexis how she came to be in her present occupation. She said:

Initially, I taught speech and language therapy. Where I grew up, you either got married or became a nurse or a teacher. I couldn't stand blood, so I became a teacher. But there are no accidents. Speech and language, communication, have always been important to me. Then I changed my work and went to Covenant House to work with kids, because I feel it's important to communicate to them that they don't have to be afraid of life.

When one fears life they most assuredly also fear death. I asked Alexis what she feels matters most in life, and how she feels about religion. I also asked her about why she feels we are here. She answered:

It's simple. We're here to love one another. We're either based out of love or based out of fear. Anything that isn't love is fear-based. I guess that's why I worked with children so much. It was always very important to me to let kids know from the start that there was nothing to fear. They didn't need to fear being deserted and they didn't need to fear failure. They simply needed to operate from a point of love and everything would be all right.

I was brought up Protestant, meaning simply that we went to Sunday school and church and everyone gossiped. Everybody was just sort of agnostic. My belief in God had nothing to do with church. It had to do with that sense, that feeling, that knowing that there was something larger than myself who created everything. I can remember lots and lots of times building penthouses with blankets, playing with my dolls, and I'd talk to God. I even did that before the accident. My sense of religion, or my sense of God, had nothing to do with that church. It had to do with animals and nature, and it had to do with looking up at the stars at night and just feeling that God existed. I knew that a Supreme Being created all that existed, and that it was love and energy. The same thing I had in me the animal had, and the tree had. I know that almost sounds druid.

I converted to Catholicism when I was thirty-six. I didn't do so because of the ritual of the Church. I did it because of the community I felt with the people that I was going to the church service with. I've always felt that it didn't matter where you prayed. Every place is a temple and everywhere is a church. Everywhere God is present. I knew that, playing with my dolls under the blankets. But I have felt, also, that man was separating himself from God through religion. Religion was creating the separateness. That always bothered me, so when I converted to Catholicism I did it with a lot of anxiety and apprehension. There was part of me drawn to it and, in retrospect, I think it was just part of a spiritual journey. I don't go to Catholic service any more.

You asked me about watches. I never had a watch until I graduated [from] high school. It never kept time for me. It just wouldn't run. In New York, sometime after I was twenty-four, I bought a watch I really liked and even painted the back of it with clear fingernail polish, thinking that then there wouldn't be a chemical reaction. But when I'd put it on the hands would just spin, so no more watches for me.

Nearly every NDEr has increased respect for, and reverence for, life. This is so even if he or she had tried to commit suicide in the past. Every experiencer confirms that life is, indeed, very precious and that what was given to us we do not have the right to destroy.

Celia had a very profound Near-Death Experience.

My accident was in 1986. I was in a head-on collision. Half of my face was totally destroyed. The eye was out of the socket. I had to have numerous surgeries. The dental will always be ongoing. I looked like I had a glass eye, but now you can't tell, after all the surgeries. I had orbital, nasal, and jaw fractures. My jaw was wired for months.

So, suddenly, I was out of my body looking down on this dead carcass. I was in the sky or the clouds, but I saw the operating room. I also saw my father and son, who looked just so lost. I was like a ghostlike thing, from the abdomen up. I had no pain. I did see through my eyes and feel through my heart.

I was up there with God, just hangin' out. God kinda had His arm around me and we were floating, upright. I was just kinda like this dangling participle. It was like how a father would hold a child. I just saw His robe, His hair and beard, and everything from His chest up. I was just hanging out there with God. He was an old great man, like a sage, a Moses-type person. I think He was my interpretation of what I thought God should look like. He was male, although I had often wondered if She would be a female. God has to have a sense of humor. He's patient, quiet, loving, adoring, stern, and definitive. There was light radiating from Him, a brightness. He had loving eyes, full beard, long hair, white robe, and love and beauty in His eyes. He was holding my hand and had His arm around me.

We had this conversation without really talking. Maybe it was telepathic. He was larger than me, but reduced to what I would conceive of as a person. It was like He was saying that everything you did in your life brought you here. You earned this. You can keep it or get rid of it. You can try to live what you have left. You can do the work that I sent you here for. In other words, He was saying that you've been screwing around with this life I gave you. You have done everything wrong and now you have to make a choice. If you want to live, then you have to live differently. You have to play by the rules. So it's like He was telling me that if I want to come back to earth, then this is what I expect of you. I felt that He was saying to me that I had been headed in the direction of ruin, and I finally got there. He asked me if He gave me more time would I do something better with my life and I said: "I'll try."

I was shown my past, and it stunk. You can't lie to yourself. But I have realized how very, very fortunate I am to have been given another chance. It ends up being a wonderful experience for me to have had this terrible accident and to have died and to have gotten in touch with God. I call him "My God," not that He isn't everyone else's, but to me it's a very personal thing. I have a wonderful feeling in my heart when I think of Him. And He's the only one who's ever really with me when everything else is crazy or awful or I'm lonely or sad or scared or nuts. I can always go to Him. I returned from there not only a fixed-up person, but a fixed person, here (pointing to her brain and heart). When He fixed this face, I believe that He also fixed my brain and my heart. I really think that was the whole thing. Everybody should really experience something awful, personally, to have this experience.

I asked Celia if she asked Him any questions. She said:

I did ask questions, but I don't remember if I verbally asked. I just felt that I would be given the answers as I deserved them. I really believed I would have to earn my return to this planet. I would have to be more thankful, more loving, kind, patient, and have more humility. I am much more thankful every day that I am here. I have so much!

I asked Celia what she thinks of life. She answered:

I think life is a gift. Some of us are lucky enough to have something terrible happen and get that smack. I think some of us kind of fumble through life and screw everybody up and themselves. I think everything in life is timing. I was there at the right time. He kind of looked at me and thought, well, let me help this poor soul out, and so I got lucky.

Belief in free will is held by the majority of Near-Death Experiencers. A very small percentage of NDErs feel that everything in our lives is predestined. Most of the subjects feel that every moment of this lifetime involves a choice. If this is so, then each and every one of us must own up to the fact that we are responsible for every moment. This relieves us of the useless energy waste of blaming others, be it the government, the society, or the proverbial "they." (Who are "they" anyway? We are they!)

NDErs and LTP experiencers, alike, confirm that one must treat their neighbor as he would want to be treated. Almost without exception, anyone who felt any degree of prejudice prior to their death experience actually came back from the other side racially colorblind. Wouldn't it be wonderful if we could gift the experience to people? Persons who "turned people off" before the episode are more accepting of others and, in turn, this attracts other people. In other words, it becomes "as you thinketh in your heart, so are you." Exactly what we put out into the universe comes back a thousandfold. When our persona is one of unconditional love, then that is exactly what we attract.

The NDErs come back knowing that we are responsible for ourselves, our actions, and our choices. We can choose to see the ugliness in another or we can choose to see them through eyes of love and light. We are all human. Therefore, we all learn by making mistakes. We don't have to like what someone else does or says, but we do have to learn that one can condemn an act without condemning the person. NDErs often come back from the other realm having learned the art of forgiveness, both of the self and of others, as well as the lesson of never judging another. We can all choose *never, never to judge.*

Most of these lessons are revealed and learned in the life review during the NDE.

Kari had a very significant life review during her second Near-Death Experience. After her return, she forgave herself for past glitches in thinking, forgave her mother and developed a renewed loving relationship with her, and came back "colorblind" with reference to race. Her story is a blessing to us all.

> I was in a bad car accident when I was twenty-two or twenty-three. I was in King of Prussia, Pennsylvania. My head went into the windshield. I remember my insides were being crushed, because they wanted to do surgery. I remember seeing the ambulance go down the road and they were arguing over what hospital to take me to. It was like, it doesn't matter guys, just pick one! I was outside the ambulance, because I could see the red light on top. I was kind of floating, and it was like I was getting lost and didn't really know where I was supposed to go next.
>
> I ended up in a tunnel and went through it. I saw my first husband in the tunnel, about midpoint. We talked and hugged. He looked exactly the same as when he died. I asked him why he didn't get any older and he told me you don't age there, that you can choose a youthful appearance. When I finally went through the tunnel Michael, an angel, started showing me things about myself.
>
> It was like, all of a sudden, there was a group bunched around me. Then they showed me things about myself. There were at least twelve entities around me. They glowed. That's when I noticed that Michael had wings. Two of the others also had wings.
>
> The first thing they showed me was how I felt about dying. I was a little angry. Scared didn't even come into it. It was like "scared" was a feeling I had no concept of. They said: "Don't worry about that. We'll come back to it." The next thing I remembered was an incident that happened with my sister. All of a sudden it was like I became my sister. I felt how angry

and hurt she had gotten over the fight we had gotten into. I saw the fight between her and me. I saw a couple of things with my mother, and it was like I became these people and literally felt hurt. There were a couple of things I could just not forgive myself for, and no amount of cajoling from this group helped. They told me it was not necessary for me to carry that, but they would honor my choice either way. When I came back from that experience I totally settled things with my mother. We became best friends after that experience.

I definitely remember seeing my spouse's death. He died by gunshot. I got to feel all of that. The beauty of it was that I not only got to experience his death, but in experiencing his, I realized that I was dying or dead. I don't know how to word it. I went through each and every experience he felt: his panic over me and his daughter and how we were going to survive without him. His love for us was just overwhelming. Then I saw and felt the gunshot and how stupid he felt about it happening. I mean, he really felt dumb! He could've avoided it, but he didn't take the precautions. It's like he was talking to me, but he wasn't. It's like I could be in multiple places at one time during this process. It was kind of bizarre how it works, but then I felt him lift from his body and how he experienced that. He felt a lot of relief. He had no fear. He kept telling me how beautiful it was and how warm, and how I would re-marry in 1980. It was like he had a telepathic connection with me at that moment, through me experiencing him. Then he told me not to grieve any more and to go on with my life. That was his last thought.

I've been truly blessed in a lot of ways. I went through a lot of things. It was very fast, the life review, and I can remember being shown things with guys I had dated. With a couple of them, I got to feel how they felt, how frustrated they were because sexually I was "uh uh, no no," and that type of thing. There was one incident in particular, where this guy was blamed for something he didn't do, and that was one of the things I had a hard time forgiving myself for. In other words, other people accused him of something and I didn't say "no" and stop it.

Then there was an incident with a girlfriend. We were probably nine or ten. She was a little older than me. We used to argue something terrible. With this incident in particular, she had gotten so angry that she stabbed my sister with a pencil. So, in retaliation, I took a flower pot and creamed her one. I went through how it felt for her to be attacked from behind like that.

There were a couple of incidents, racially, that totally took away any feeling I had toward racism. Color doesn't mean a thing to me now, and it hasn't for years. This woman was petrified. It was during our high school years. We were fourteen. She was teasing me. It made her feel big to do this, because she felt so small, and so it was "pick on the new kid in school" type of thing and show her who's boss. I got that attitude plus I got the total shock and surprise when I turned around and slugged her. She really wanted to burst out crying, but didn't. And I saw where her feelings mirrored my own. Here I was the new kid in school, and had never been around a black person, let alone gone to school with any. Because I grew up in a very sheltered neighborhood when I was little, going to an all-black school just petrified me. So I was shown how she was also petrified and we tended to work things through, because I stood my ground. She and I ended up becoming friends after a while. But it was like I saw how she felt about our friendship, too, and how intense it was for her.

Then they took me through some other things from childhood, basically teaching me not to be envious, not to be judgmental, not to put other things before me as more important, meaning material things, possessions, that type of thing. It was almost like I was being shown the Ten Commandments, but in a very odd way. It ended up with my birth, which was "Honor thy father and thy mother." My mother, when she was giving birth to me, was held off because the doctor wasn't there yet, so I heard and felt everything that went through her

mind while she was in the delivery room. I heard her screaming: "Get this kid out of me. It's killing me. It's killing me!"—
all that kind of stuff. Up until that point I could never do
enough to please my mother, and I could never understand
why I felt that way. But after this Near-Death it changed, and
my mother said: "You know, we're finally friends." I told her
that I honored her space and I realize that she had feelings,
too. I remember the conversation very well.

I asked Kari if she actually remembered the physical feeling of
being in the womb. She answered:

> Yes. It was frightening. I felt my fear and I felt my mother's
> fear, because even though she was yelling and screaming, she
> was also worried that maybe something would be wrong with
> me. Then when I came out they all went "uh" and my mother
> said "What?" and they didn't say anything. So it was like I was
> looking through her eyes down at me and thinking: "What an
> ugly child!" I was born with a veil on my face.
>
> After I had the review, I remember feeling the light, almost
> like it was calling me. I turned and walked into it. I felt
> vibrant, alive, really alive. It was pure, pure love. It has wis-
> dom. It has consciousness. It definitely is us. It told me I
> could stay sheltered there and I said: "I really can't. I'm really
> worried about Tom, my friend who is ill." And with that,
> BAM, I was back!

It is true that forgiveness is divine. It certainly is divine when we as
humans learn to forgive not only others who have done Less-Than-
Positive things to us, but also forgive ourselves. Those victims of violent crime who are blessed to have a deep core Near-Death Experience or an out-of-body experience often demonstrate the ability to
rise above the usual resultant negative human emotions. This results
from remarkable spiritual growth. The type of experience that occurs
appears to be determined by the victim's soul's desire or need, both of
which my be conscious or subconscious. When the experience occurs

during childhood, as a means of escaping various physical or emotional abuses, it often sets that child on a lifelong spiritual quest. The feeling of being bathed in the pure, unconditional love in that living, loving, bright, white, God light, and the learning of the lesson of forgiveness (both of the perpetrator and of the self) are but two of the divine gifts that may be received by the victim.

Priscilla is a well-educated, lovely lady who had a Near-Death Experience following a cardiac arrest secondary to a massive heart attack. As a young child she was sexually abused by an older brother. Despite many, many years of all the various therapies: psychotherapy, group therapy, hypnotherapy, even biofeedback, she was unable to rid herself of feelings of overwhelming guilt and overwhelming shame. Her NDE was certainly the nexus point of her life. She tells her story next.

> In 1991, when I was forty-seven years old, I was admitted to the hospital with symptoms of a heart attack. I got nauseated, passed out, and "coded"—heart beat and breathing stopped. Actually, I coded three times. It was as if it wasn't happening to me. I could hear the doctors arguing about the care they were going to give me. When I came out of my body, one of the doctors was straddling me on the table doing the CPR (cardiopulmonary resuscitation) so I went right through him! Then there was this other voice that was saying that it was going to be okay. It was a voice that was further off. It was a quiet, calming, soft, and soothing voice, so I felt real calm. I looked down and saw my husband, daughter, and son, all crying. I kept trying to say to them: "It'll be okay. I'm okay."
>
> I went into this big, bright light. Believe me, I'm a changed person since that happened. I'm not at all the same. That real bright light was golden, with a rosy hue. There was soft, operatic type music. Now, since then, I love opera and never used to. I did have a flashback and started to panic.

Priscilla was very emotional when she told me about her life review. Instead of seeing a panorama of every second of her lifetime, and instead of seeing multiple pictures of single events, she was shown one thing and one thing only. She was shown the sexual abuse. She relived it. The Supreme Entity, who facilitated this, lovingly said to her only one sentence, telepathically: "My child, it was *not* your fault!" That one sentence from that loving, nonjudgmental presence did what all of those years of therapy couldn't do. It liberated her from her fear, liberated her from her guilt, liberated her from her shame, bathed her in unconditional love, and gave her back her self-esteem. Her healing was instantaneous!

She says she has changed in many, many ways.

> I know there is a real purpose for me being here. Heaven isn't ready for me yet. I'm not vain as I used to be, with reference to my appearance. I always used to be worried about my hair, nails, makeup, and clothes. They all had to be just so. Now I'm just me. Material things aren't important any more. And I wasn't really brought up in any religion, but went to Sunday school at a Nazarene church, then got married in a Catholic church. Now we've joined a Mennonite church. God sent me there. See, I'm NOT the same person. Another thing is that death was always frightening to me until this happened. It's not now, because that was a touch of heaven. It was the warmth I felt and that comforting voice. I'll tell you something else. Since then, I'll awaken in the middle of the night and words will be flooding out of me, which is poetry. I never wrote poetry before.

The brother who abused Priscilla died many years before the Near-Death Experience. She had never confronted him, and had never been able to forgive him, let alone herself. She is now free because she has total forgiveness in her heart. That wonderful experience gave her just exactly what she needed!

Kara was brutally murdered in a home invasion, and was resuscitated by the police and fire rescue personnel. Despite the horrible brutality, this dear lady has actually forgiven the perpetrator! She tells her fascinating story:

> It happened in 1993, in Florida, when I was thirty-six. Even though I was a nurse in California, I was working as a nurse's aide since I didn't have a Florida license. I lived in a little ramshackle house, very secluded from the street. I used to feed all the cats in the neighborhood. At 11:30 one night I went out back to feed them. When I came back into the house I remember turning the deadbolt, because it makes so much noise. I walked into the kitchen, and there was a man in front of the stove! He lives around the corner. I'd seen him before, and knew he was bad news. He was definitely there to rape me and kill me. He had a rifle, a knife, and a flashlight. So it was premeditated, first degree. My kitchen knife was on the drainboard. I picked it up and swiped at him. We obviously struggled through the dining room and living room. I don't remember what happened after that, including the first blow, but I've seen the crime scene photos and my memory stopped where most of the blood was.

Because I would like it to still remain "unimaginable" what was done with the rifle and knife, only a part of that portion of the interview is repeated here.

> He took the butt of the rifle and smashed it into my face which fractured, as well as my sinuses, nose, both my eye sockets and my head, my jaw, and my teeth. He also hit my shoulder with the rifle and left an imprint of an "S", like a scroll. I was stabbed seven times in the face, and he obviously succeeded in cutting out my right eye. Then he strangled me, and his fingerprints were on my neck. It was knife and rifle wounds elsewhere that caused perforated intestines and hemorrhage, which was the actual cause of death.

Apparently the man next door heard the inhuman screams and called the police. My attacker is a deaf mute, and ran out just as the police were rounding the corner. What flipped the cops out was seeing my teeth laying on the floor and my eye hanging out. Anyway, I was resuscitated, and later I had to have a tracheotomy.

I guess it's while I was dead that I went through this brief tunnel thing, and then was in this place that was so incredibly beautiful! It was vibrant and living, and the colors were so beautiful! Wow! There were real vibrant green leaves and pink and rose-pink flowers, like a trellis. They were like a backdrop, everywhere, like an arch in all of my vision. These were no ordinary flowers. These were IMAX, 3D, technicolor.

Then came a man, just an ordinary man, dressed in a white and black suit or tuxedo. He was regular sized, with a beard and mustache and dark hair. He was very welcoming and communicated with me by thought. He might have been a guide. He said: "We're glad you're here. We have a lot of work for you to do." We went on together. I must've been floating, because it was all cloudy stuff, nothing firm to walk on. We go into this room that didn't have any walls. It was like cloudy, foamy stuff. In this room there's a very, very old switchboard with all these lines that you plug in. It was very big and very grand. I could hear a woman praying down below to break her daughter's fever. There were three ladies answering the lines. They had long honey-colored hair, no wings. You couldn't see much of them, because they were sitting. One had a kind of a deep rose-pink colored dress, but the fabric covered a large part of her so I couldn't tell if she had legs. They weren't talking. It was like a communications thing where they plug in a line and the entity or angel, or whatever, goes down to the right place to work on that prayer. It was a prayer switchboard!

The guide said to me: "We really need you here." I told him I didn't know, because my family needed me, too. After a while, he said: "All right, you can go back, but you have to speak." Well, I haven't shut up since!

I asked Kara what she took with her from the experience, and what changes she has undergone because of it. She answered:

> I learned there is so much more that we don't know. Hey, if I'm needed there, then anyone can make it there. All that stuff about sin and forgiveness and that He died for sins is hogwash. You guys are really off the mark. Since that happened, I don't judge people and everyone looks the same to me.
>
> That man who attacked me? Well, I had forgiven him long before the State Attorney put him away. He was a prior felon, who was released from prison too early because of overcrowding. He had violently raped another woman and also kidnapped her. It wasn't like I love him, but he played a part in my life. People do play parts in our lives. What can we say? He was a product of society. He was a felon since he was seventeen years old, so he can't do anything else. That's what he does. Our paths crossed.
>
> The Near-Death Experience that I had was a gift, even with all that pain, being disfigured, losing my teeth, and everything else. If I could go back in time and rewind, knowing he's gonna smash me, stab me, do all those horrible things, horrible pain, many surgeries, but also this unbelievable Near-Death Experience, would I choose it again? Yes, in a heartbeat! It was a true gift!

Kara admits that she would have felt tremendous bitterness, and would not have been able to forgive her would-be murderer, had it not been for the NDE. She remains physically disfigured. She continues to grow spiritually on a daily basis. Her psychic abilities have increased, geometrically, especially in the area of receiving information about murders that are in the news. Her new endeavor will be to organize a national association for victims of violent crime.

Candice Lee is another very spiritual lady who was brutally attacked and strangled. She was twenty-one years old at the time. She, too, has forgiven her would-be murderer.

I was picking my husband up from work at the nightclub, about 1 A.M. He wasn't outside like he was supposed to be, so I was waiting in the car. All of a sudden a black man comes out of nowhere, pulls me out of the car, drags me a couple of houses down, and proceeds to strangle me to death. He murdered me. He, indeed, murdered me!

I heard a loud, buzzing sound and then I was in total blackness. Then I went through a tunnel. Three angels pulled me up the tunnel to the light at the other end. When we first arrived I saw my dad! He had died when I was fifteen. There was a whole bunch of other people there, too. I knew they were my family, but I didn't actually know them. They were in a gigantic room that seemed like it went on forever. There were no walls. There was the brightest light you could imagine, brighter than sunlight.

Then the angels flew me to this room that had pillars all around it and glass windows. There was a table with a book on it. I'm almost 5'4", and the table was so high that I could barely see over it. The angels were gigantic, huge, probably 15 feet tall. The table was very long. The book was open on one end of the table. I stood at the side of the table, and there was an angel on either side of me. There was another angel standing over the book. The book was humongous. It was about three feet tall when open. The angel flipped through this book and found my page. All of a sudden, these two angels whisked me up and flew me right in front of the book and one said: "See, this is your page."

Then they flew me out of there and right into another room, right in front of Jesus! There I was, kneeling down, and they were standing on either side of me. Well, He comes down off this gold platform, walks down to me, and then He said to me: "Go back. It is not yet your time. You are to teach." Jesus looked like you or me, except that He shined. He was nothing but pure light, but I could see His body. He had on a white robe. I could see His face. His hair was pure light. His whole being was light. He glowed! There's nothing on earth as great.

The love enveloped all around me. You can *feel* it and it's everywhere.

The floor looked like mother of pearl and there were big, white, Roman-type columns with swirls around them. They were gigantic and looked like they were made of white marble. There were a lot of other people, like from days of old, dressed in old clothes. They weren't see-through, and they didn't shine.

After Jesus told me it wasn't my time, I shot back down that tunnel and landed in my body with a clang. It was a sound like you'd imagine a jail cell door would sound like being slammed. I opened my eyes and the black man was standing over me. He was horrified and freaked out. He kept saying: "You were dead!" I think I was gone about fifteen minutes, far beyond the limit they allow you to be dead and still come back normal. I put my hands in a praying position and said: "For God's sake, leave me alive!" I really wanted to stay in heaven and not come back, but God doesn't give you a choice.

Finally, the ambulance and police came. I was a mess after that for some time. My eyes were bulging out when he was strangling me. They felt like they'd pop right out of my head. I had black and blue marks around my throat for nearly six months.

If that experience hadn't happened, then I would've never seen the Lord. I would've never gone to heaven and I wouldn't have seen my Dad. It was supposed to happen. It was supposed to wake me up. When my father died I took my Bible, screamed at the top of my lungs: "God, you don't exist," threw the Bible across the room and never looked back. When this happened it woke me up. Now I know that my father's spirit still lives. Now I know that God gives us free will and we can make our lives lousy or good. We can do horrible things or good things. I came away with the knowledge that I'm supposed to teach, not high school, but about the Lord. Now every day of my life I say: "Lord, use me. I'm an open channel for you to use," and He does.

I've forgiven my murderer. I pray for him that he comes to know the Lord. When we can have the love and compassion of both men and women in our souls, then we will become one with the Lord. Being here is only a test to see what we're made of. Let's face it, some people are horrible and yet they're beautiful. There's both sides here. We've got the best of the best and the worst of the worst in this world.

Candice Lee had profound life-altering changes, which took time to manifest. She feels absolute forgiveness for her attacker. The Near-Death Experience certainly opened her up to other spiritually transforming events. She has had several occasions where she saw angels. She has recently changed jobs and is now caring for the mentally handicapped. In her NDE she received not only what she wanted (seeing her father) but also what she needed (confirmation that the Lord exists).

TEN

Conclusions: Plea to the Medical Community

As we have seen, there is a bonanza of fascinating experiences, many of which we have shared. I wish I could have presented them all in this first offering. Whether the experience was perceived as Less-Than-Positive or as a peaceful and joyous affirmation of unconditional love, the profound happening irreversibly changed the person. The life-altering changes can be as significant or even more life-altering for the LTP experiencer than for the prototypical NDEr. Most, after dealing with the immediate issues of coming back into a possibly painful traumatized body, eventually deal with the reasons they saw, felt, or heard what they did. They then usually experience a decreased fear of death, a renewed veneration for life, increased warmth for family and friends, increased spirituality, increased thirst for knowledge—seeking wisdom, a decreased interest in material things,

A candle loses none of its flame by lighting another candle.

—Kelly

and the affirmation that the most important reason for our being here is to learn and practice unconditional love for every human being. They often develop a "live and let live" attitude, realizing that everyone is on their own path. Not only do most learn never, never to judge, but learn the even more divine lesson of forgiving not only others, but themselves as well. They know what is right and what is wrong in an absolute sense. Most learn to live in the moment, and savor each one. Some become risk takers, they "just do it." Everyone doesn't necessarily take a walk on the wild side, because some become even more cautious than before their Near-Death Experience. It is variable.

In summary, there are basically three reasons why a Less-Than-Positive experience occurs instead of, or in addition to, a blissful light NDE. First, the LTP event is an impetus to reevaluate previous choices, actions, reactions, thoughts, and belief systems. Second, an LTP event may occur because the person's mindset immediately prior to the experience was less than loving. Third, I feel that many of the examples have proven that an LTP may occur secondary to negative programming during childhood. When one grows up programmed to expect hell fire and brimstone, then that is what projected to the cosmos and that is exactly what one may experience.

Most of the Less-Than-Positive experiences end up being true learning experiences. All of the subjects in my study group, with no exception, learned to change behavior that "doesn't work" to that which does work. Bart Ostroff, hypnotherapist, teacher, friend and mentor says that "self-awareness without change is self-abuse." The LTP experiencers, for the most part, stop their self-abuse once they understand that what they were shown was needed for that purpose. They do, indeed, adjust their attitudes if that was needed, and adjust glitches in their belief systems if that was needed.

I shall reiterate my hypothesis about who or what determines that which we see, hear and feel in the experience, be it a Less-Than-

Positive one or a joyful one. We are the ones who determine this. It is our very consciousness, essence, soul, spirit, or life force, that projects what it is that we *need* to endure. If it is something that we need to *shock* us into change, then that is what we project and that is what we are shown. Remember, the cosmic forces, including a supreme entity, can certainly "read" our needs.

Once we are on the other plane, we are pure thought. When we are released from our shell, or garment (physical body), we become energy. As discussed previously, energy is information. Therefore, in the initial portion of the LTP or NDE, we are the transmitters of our wants and needs, whether they are conscious or subconscious. It is the cosmic forces, "the One," the ultimate, the supreme being, our guardian angels, our guides, our deceased relatives, whoever, that are the initial receivers of this information. Then, as the event progresses, we become the receivers and those entities become the transmitters.

Our needs will far outweigh and take precedence over our wants. We may *want* to see a particular loved one, but if the *need* we project is for a lesson to be learned or for certain knowledge to be obtained, then that is what will be shown to us in the way that will best get our attention. I believe that explains why some experiences begin as "positive" and then change into Less-Than-Positive and vice versa. Since our thoughts, even while going through the experience, continue to be projected as energy, what we are shown will be individual and according to our own model of the world (primarily visual, auditory or kinesthetic). This may partially explain why some people *see* their deceased loved ones, why some people *hear* heavenly music, why some people *smell* their deceased loved one, and why some people come back having been *told* significant universal knowledge.

Our ultimate need (that which will make a significant difference in how we continue to live this present life time more meaningfully) is ultimately what we are shown. Although the need surpasses the want, both can certainly be satisfied in an NDE. It's an "ask and ye shall receive" deal, whether we realized we were asking or not. Those of you who think that you are the center of the universe and think that you determine your destiny are probably right. Those of you who feel that a supreme being determines all that happens to you are also right. Actually you are both right. It is just semantics. Nearly everyone who has had one of these experiences tells us that we are all connected, not only to each other, but to the supreme being. Subjectively, that feels right to me.

What a child I was at the beginning of this project. I remember actually saying to my husband that I have all my questions ready for when I have my NDE or LTP. How silly! Now I know that I don't have to voice anything! It is an all-knowing. The cosmic forces, higher power, collective consciousness, whatever term we are comfortable with, of course already knows what I need to have answered or be shown. I would certainly bet my eternity on the fact that when I am separated from this physical garment I will project my need and desire to see my husband, Sonny, and my father, J. Jay, and they will be there. So the only thing I will try to remember to tell myself when I find that I'm in the experience, is to just let go and flow. I do have that *trust* (key word) and *knowing* (another key word) that my needs and probably my wants will be satisfied. It all probably boils down to the very biggest key word of all: *faith*.

I hope that I have been able to show anyone who has had an LTP episode that they are certainly not alone. Every single one of us might join you in a similar experience some day if the *need* is there. We all have made some less-than-positive choices because we are human. I believe wholeheartedly that if we do our life review and soul search on this side now, acknowledging those erroneous choices, then we might not have to go through it again on the other side. Faulty belief systems and errors in judgment or reasoning can certainly be amended here. Christopher M. Bache stated: "If there is a lesson to be learned from these encounters, it is a lesson that we must learn collectively not just individually . . . we have some precedent for thinking that when a member of a species brings some aspect of its collective anguish into conscious awareness, it has a healing effect that is distributed through the species as a whole." I agree. Forgiveness is certainly one of those lessons. When we forgive ourselves and others, then we all experience healing.

Plea to the Medical Community

I feel compelled to make a special plea to everyone in the medical community, including all physicians, all nurses, all emergency response personnel and every single hospital, nursing home and medical office employee. IANDS, the International Association for Near-Death Studies, has suggested some guidelines for dealing with NDErs. They suggest being sensitive to the fact that during a resuscitative effort, the patient may very well be hearing and seeing everything that is going on. This may also be so when one is in coma. Please act as though he or she can hear and see you, and do not make any less-than-positive comments.

After the person is resuscitated, ask him if he remembers anything during the time that he was unconscious. If he says he does not, then drop the issue, of course. If he does recall an experience, then please assure him confidentiality and allow him, with respectful listening, to relate the experience and express his emotions. Assure him that these experiences are not uncommon, but that every one is unique in some aspects, because every human being is unique. Be sensitive to his interpretation of the event. Some people, for example, will interpret it as a religious experience, others as a spiritual experience, etc. Allow him his own interpretation, please, since he was there and we were not.

Please do not automatically refer the person for psychiatric care or in any way give the person the impression that his episode was a pathologic symptom. If you are uncomfortable listening to one of these accounts, and cannot be objective, then please find someone who is comfortable. There are IANDS support groups, such as South Florida IANDS, all over the country and in other parts of the world. If you are willing to hear these accounts, then please ask the patient if you may discuss it with his family, specifically to inform them that it is a common occurrence. That will deepen their understanding. We must be our patients' best patient advocates, in all spheres, meaning the mind, body, and spirit.

I am begging you all to never, never tell your patient that their experience was not real. Do not tell them it was a hallucination, delusion, drug-induced, endorphin-related, etc. Of course, give them any information you feel is appropriate if they ask. If we deny the person's experience, and their perception of their experience, then we invalidate both the experience and the person. I must reiterate that if we invalidate a patient's spirituality, then I can assure you that we invalidate our own.

I must admit that for some time I was very, very concerned about how to convince my peers that the Near-Death Experience and other related events are valid. I now realize that this is not my purpose. I have come to accept that without my help, if not within this lifetime then certainly in death, everyone will come to that realization. Until one does have a Near-Death Experience, another type of spiritually transforming event or death, all of my attempts to convince will be pointless. I know that when one's soul is ready, that spiritually transforming event will occur. Who knows? That event may even be running across a book such as this, that simply speaks to one's heart and soul from another person's heart and soul.

Epilogue

*I*n reviewing this book I would hope that the medical community, which has traditionally been wedded to an empirical scientific world view, will consider this work non-judgmentally and with an open-mindedness of its vast possibilities. Western medicine focuses a great deal of its time and energy heroically trying to cover up for, and thus maintain, and heal diseases that are the result of the very scientific/economic system out of which it was born.

Holding on to old belief systems in the name of science is often very emotional and based more on the politics as well as the economics. Unlike the medical model, which believes that healing comes from the ability to scientifically define mechanisms, Dr. Rommer's personal and professional journey has openly explored a sure-to-be controversial area. Her gutsy study of the NDE (Near-Death Experience) will, at the very least, allow the medical community to reconsider their grandiose assumptions about theory, technique, and practice. Dr. Rommer's visionary beliefs into the never-never are quite prophetic, and she is to be congratulated for her courageous spiritual exploration on Near-Death Experiences.

Helping people survive at a different level of comfort, apart from medication, is certainly available to everyone. The very thoughts that people put in their minds are as significant as the foods, vitamins, and medications being applied. In fact, at best, the medical establishment is still linked to what implies an inherent mind-body split, rather than a mind-body connection. Both logical and linear medical science is objective so, by definition, NDE does not really exist. Medical science has dismissed many experiences encountered by patients that are not measurable to what they can predict and thus control. The subjective experiences of so many people who have undergone NDEs describe entirely different accounts beyond science. In this book, Dr. Rommer has eloquently come out to describe this vital subject as opposed to winning the approval of her peers.

Does it really matter whether Near-Death Experiences or Less-Than-Positive experiences exist, so long as they offer a different perception of death, particularly for those who live with deep-seated fears? Medical science has evolved into a need to deny our own experiences and our own perception in order to fit into an ideology with the usual conclusion being hallucination or impossibility. After all, medical dominance borders on what is rational, analytical, and intellectual. It can often be arrogant and grandiose.

Dr. Rommer's book is both valid and important, because it connects us to our spirituality. When will the "pure sciences" realize that people crave objectivity, because to be subjective is to be vulnerable to our beliefs. Perhaps the problem within the scientific approach to medicine is that it creates a mindset interaction which completely ignores and thus never questions things such as the placebo effect, the power of prayer in healing, and even remission. It is not as though the scientific medical model has not had a budding awareness of these phenomena, but rather have repetitiously discounted their value to the patient's benefit. As long as medicine is solely linked to the cure of disease with drugs and surgery, excluding all else with an "inconsequential, it's beyond me" attitude, unimagined transformation will remain status quo.

Perhaps true healing can flexibly encompass and trust the results of what many have shared within the contents of this book. The scientific medical model robs people of the possibility of claiming ownership of their lives, and often prevents what we need to do within ourselves to allow healing to occur. Perhaps this book will open a new vanguard of understanding far more than what science is too quick to figure out.

Spirituality is an unexplained "given" that's not about bad or good. It just is. As we learn more of what many have come to experience, we can then integrate the results into a new evolving process of understanding. Dr. Rommer's book is a clarion call which has sounded a defined need for the medical profession to embrace a new kind of total healing that is necessary for our country and our planet. Dr. Rommer's work is certainly "worth its salt" and probably will generate more questions than has been answered. This book represents an opportunity to remove the mystery, concerns, and questions, and open a new vision of possibility.

Just as true love lives on when earthly things die, spirit and soul also soar beyond all knowing.

—Bart Ostroff
Fort Lauderdale, Florida
September, 1997

Afterword

$\mathcal{A}$lbert Einstein said: "The effort to get at the truth has to precede all other efforts." I think it is important to share with you a personal communication that I had with long time near-death researcher and author, P. M. H. Atwater. This was immediately after the first printing of the book, but before its release to the public. She has interviewed many Less Than Positive experiencers, and points out her different and valid conclusions. Difference of opinion is, to me, crucial to report. I must also point out again that all near-death research is dependent upon who is willing to come forward and discuss their experience. P. M. H. Atwater wrote:

> I am very excited about what you have done with this study, and I am very proud of you. This type of work is sorely needed in the field of near-death studies. My only regret is that I did not know you were about to publish. Had I known, your contribution would have been given coverage in my book, *The Complete Idiot's Guide to Near-Death Experiences* (Macmillan; Indianapolis, IN, 2000). Also, you needed to know about my work with child experiencers of near-death states, contained in *Children of the New Millennium* (Three Rivers Press: New York

City, 1999). Since we somehow missed an opportunity to dialogue, allow me to interject a few thoughts now. Perhaps you can put them to good use.

In reading *Blessing in Disguise,* I noticed that the experiencers interviewed were able to find meaning in what happened to them, and, for the most part, successfully integrate their episode into their daily life. That was not true with those I found in my research. Of the 3,000 adult and 277 child experiencers with whom I have had sessions, 15 percent of the adults and 3 percent of the children had what I call unpleasant and/or hellish episodes. Positive integration was about 50/50—half did, half didn't.

I'll never forget the fellow I met in Las Vegas, Nevada, who walked up to me as I was signing books in the open space of a busy Mall. He had rigid body language, his face stern and serious. He stretched out his right arm, then pointed right at me, glaring as he did, and yelled: "You got to tell people there's a hell. All them pretty stories about heaven and love aren't true. There's a hell and I've been there and it isn't pretty at all. Them love and light people are liars. That's not the way it is."

We had quite a talk afterward. I listened intently and what I heard was fear. He just couldn't accept what happened to him during his near-death scenario as compared to the other stories experiencers were telling. He seemed empowered by the terror he experienced and he clung to his fear as if he had earned the right to feel it. His mind was completely closed to interpreting his scenario in any other manner than literally. I noticed that he seemed to need the power his fear gave him—the power to be different, to hurt deep inside without having to face why or what he could do to heal. It was as if his fear protected him from taking responsibility for his life.

Although unpleasant experiences can be instructive and positive in the illuminations and healings that may result, not everyone can deal with them. The same is true with the more uplifting, pleasant kind. These also can be traumatic to handle. I am working right now with a woman consumed with anger for having to come back, yet also assailed with guilt that she'd rather be on the other side of death than with her children.

One thing I've learned in over two decades of researching near-death experiences—is that we cannot make absolute statements about any aspect of the phenomenon. No matter what we conjecture or conclude, there is always an exception, another way of looking at the situation.

First and foremost, we must honor the other person's truth. And we have not done that with child experiencers of near-death states. We revel in "out-of-the-mouth-of-babes" stories without ever taking the time to study the impact of what they went through or how they interpret what happened to them. Nor do we track the aftereffects through their growing years. We see them through adult eyes and compare them with adult models, bypassing minds too young to recognize what we do. I attempted to correct this oversight with *Children of the New Millennium*, and I'd like to make yet another correction here.

Somehow a very important case was edited out of the book during its rewrite stages, being mentioned only in brief on page 70 and even there a major error was overlooked. I am speaking of Judith Werner, Bronx (now of Brooklyn), New York, who, when nine days old (not nine, implying "years," as it says in my book), was operated on for a serious staph infection and abscess. She experienced a near-death episode during surgery which consisted of white-suited figures, devoid of emotion, standing around her, with a huge light glaring down from above.

The drawing she made for me (when she was an adult) shows in the upper half what you and I would consider the typical layout and personnel found in any modern hospital, and is accompanied by her written description: A baby is lying in "a crib or incubator with [a] plastic bubble top. [There is a] large bright white light—from the ceiling or hanging from above. Several white-suited figures, more of them women than men [stand beside the crib]. They appear very large." The lower half of her drawing shows her as an older child continuing to receive treatments for the infection that nearly killed her as an infant. These treatments consisted of a special light: "In some dreams a very bright goosenecked lamp irradiates me—although I am not a baby. The gooseneck ray lamp that appears in other dreams also illuminating from above and from right side. A large powerful woman directing [the] process, or just a voice is heard." She described it as being administered by the same type of white-suited "zombie" as before.

Because her drawings depict the cold sterility of ordinary medical environments, it is easy to dismiss her case as simple memory. But if you really listen to experiencers, study them, surprising details often emerge, as they did in Judith's case. To her infant eyes these white-clad figures were evil giants, the light a torture, her subsequent treatments more akin to punishment. Plus, there was another component to her episode. Along with the visual imagery, a heavy voice spoke, that seemed to her as if a man threatening her. This "Inner Stranger" was exceedingly demanding of her behavior if she was to survive.

Once verbal, she told her parents about the incident and about the Inner Stranger and what he said. They pooh-poohed her story. She told other friends and relatives, and was also rebuffed. She then repressed the episode and said nothing more, until, at age twenty-eight, she had a near-death-like experience that explained what happened to her during surgery when she was only nine days old. The closure she received from the second episode enabled her to understand lingering childhood fears and angers, and she began the process of turning her life around in a positive manner.

Before we go further in our discussion of this case, we must ask ourselves: how could a nine-day-old infant clearly remember surgical details as Judith did? How could such an infant respond to and retain the words of a threatening male? Throughout her entire life?

Judith has an unusually high IQ, which is typical with child experiencers. Eventually, she developed her psychic sensitivity to the point that she became professional in her ability to advise others in solving their own problems. The sternness of her early near-death state, even being lectured and threatened, is similar to childhood cases from Asia and various Third World countries, as well as native peoples (regardless of tribal affiliation). Occasionally, I have encountered episodes like this with children from industrialized nations (as was Judith).

It is apparent to me that we, as a society, need to reconsider research findings of brain development in newborns and toddlers. Half of the child experiencers in my research base, for instance, could remember their birth, one-third had prebirth memory, and most of those that I could verify, via their mothers' testimony, began remembering at around seven months in utero, the same time medical science tells us that the fetus can feel and respond to pain.

We also need to reconsider the power of near-death states and how even simple incidents can have powerful effects; how individuals can and often do have multiple episodes that seem somehow to build on each other, or challenge and stretch experiencers even further than the original one. Because there is so much more we need to know, I am grateful to you, Barbara, for daring to go that extra step—exploring in areas many others have ignored or avoided.

—P. M. H. Atwater, Lh.D.

Bibliography

Atwater, P. M. H. *Beyond the Light*. New York: Avon Books, 1994.

———. "Is There a Hell? Surprising Observations About the Near-Death Experience." *Journal of Near-Death Studies*, 10, 149–160, 1991.

Bache, C. M. "Expanding Grof's Concept of the Perinatal: Deepening the Inquiry into Frightening Near-Death Experiences." *Journal of Near-Death Studies*, 15, 115–139, 1996.

Baily, L. "Nihilism and No-Thingness in the NDE." Paper presented at the North American Conference of the International Association for Near-Death Studies, 1996.

Brooks, Michael. *Instant Rapport*. New York: Warner Books, 1989.

Bush, Nancy E. "Frightening NDEs." Paper presented at the North American Conference of the International Association for Near-Death Studies, 1996.

Campbell, Joseph. *The Portable Jung*. New York: Penguin Books, 1971.

Cuthrell, Jack. *Letters of the Soul . . . From the Silence of the Mind.* Tequesta, Florida: Spiritual Quest, 1995.

Ellwood, Gracia F. "Distessing Near-Death Experiences as Photographic Negatives." *Journal of Near-Death Studies*, 15, 83–114, 1996.

Frankl, Viktor E. *Man's Search for Meaning.* New York: Simon & Schuster, 1959.

Gallup, G., Jr., and W. Proctor. *Adventures in Immortality: A Look Beyond the Threshold of Death.* New York: McGraw-Hill, 1982.

Greyson, Bruce, and Nancy Evans Bush. "Distressing Near-Death Experiences." *Psychiatry*, 55: 95–110, 1992.

Jaegers, Bevy. "NDE: The Black Hole Phenomenon." *Vital Signs*, 15, No. 2, 13–14, 1996.

Kushner, Harold S. *How Good Do We Have to Be?* New York: Little, Brown & Co., 1996.

Langlois, Carole Sanborne. *Soul Rescue: Help on the Way Home to Spirit.* Fort Lauderdale, Florida: That's the Spirit Publishing Company, 1993.

Moody, Raymond A., Jr. *Life After Life.* Simons Island, Georgia: Mockingbird, 1975.

———. *Reflections on Life After Life.* Simons Island, Georgia: Mockingbird, 1977.

Morse, Melvin, and P. Perry. *Closer to the Light: Learning from the Near Death Experiences of Children.* New York: Random House, 1990.

———. *Transformed by the Light.* New York: Ballantine Books, 1992.

Rawlings, M. *Beyond Death's Door.* Nashville: Thomas Nelson, Inc., 1978.

Ring, Kenneth. *Heading Toward Omega: In Search of the Meaning of the Near-Death Experience.* New York: Morrow, 1984.

———. *Life at Death: A Scientific Investigation of the Near-Death Experience.* New York: Coward, McCann and Georghegan, 1980.

———. "Solving the Riddle of Frightening Near-Death Experiences: Some Testable Hypotheses and a Perspective Based on A Course in Miracles." *Journal of Near-Death Studies*, 13, 5–23, 1994.

Rommer, Barbara R., M.D. "The Near-Death Experience as a Gateway to Higher Consciousness: God is Within." The Academy of Religion and Psychical Research, *1998 Annual Conference Proceedings.* 96–104, 1998.

Sabom, Michael. *Recollections of Death: A Medical Investigation.* New York: Harper and Row, 1982.

Serdahely, William J. "Variations From the Prototypic Near-Death Experience: The 'Individually Tailored' Hypothesis." *Journal of Near-Death Studies*, 13, 186–196, 1995.

Sharp, Kimberly Clark. *After the Light.* New York: Avon Books, 1995.

Watson, Lyall. *Lifetide.* New York: Simon & Schuster, 1979.

☽ REACH FOR THE MOON

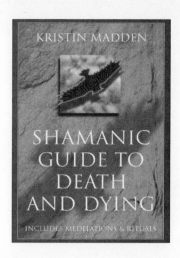

SHAMANIC GUIDE TO DEATH AND DYING
Includes Meditations & Rituals

Kristin Madden

Throughout history and across the globe, societies have called upon their shamans to assist the dying, the dead, and those loved ones remaining in physical life. The shaman, as death-walker, is responsible for guiding us through our journeys to the next world. This book, written by a modern shamanic deathwalker, offers personal experience and practical examples of the process through life into death and rebirth, along with suggested methods for you to use in your own experience.

The Shamanic Guide to Death and Dying will take you on a journey beyond this reality. It will show you the continuity of life after the death of the physical body, and will help you to reconnect with departed loved ones and your own spirit guides.

- Find out what really happens at the moment of death, and to what worlds we travel after leaving this body
- Experience actual deathwalks for humans and animals through the eyes and ears of modern deathwalkers
- Explore your own past lives and learn about the effects of other lives on your current incarnation
- Create and facilitate rites of passage and other ceremonies using the outlines provided
- Find out why children are more open to the Other worlds and how to encourage their abilities and self-esteem
- Learn to assist your pets through their passages

1-56718-494-4, 288 pp., 7½ x 9⅛   **$16.95**

MESSAGES AND MIRACLES
Extraordinary Experiences of the Bereaved

Louis E. LaGrand, Ph.D.

In this moving and compassionate work, one of the pioneers in after-death communication (ADC) research explores the reasons why ADCs occur and how they help the bereaved.

Based on his counseling experience, interviews with numerous people who have had contact with a deceased loved one, and the many questions people have asked him since the the release of his first book, *After Death Communication*, LaGrand unfolds an untapped source of support for the bereaved and those who attempt to comfort them.

Learn whether contact experience is simply the stress of bereavement or an authentic communication, how it can help you establish a new relationship with the deceased, and how to talk to children who report the experience. Read actual accounts of ADCs which have never before appeared in print.

1-56718-406-5, 336 pp., 6 x 9, illus.   **$12.95**

TRUE HAUNTINGS
Spirits with a Purpose

Hazel M. Denning, Ph.D.

Do spirits feel and think? Does death automatically promote them to a paradise—or as some believe, a hell? Real-life ghostbuster Dr. Hazel M. Denning reveals the answers through case histories of the friendly and hostile earthbound spirits she has encountered. Learn the reasons spirits remain entrapped in the vibrational force field of the earth: fear of going to the other side, desire to protect surviving loved ones, and revenge. Dr. Denning also shares fascinating case histories involving spirit possession, psychic attack, mediumship and spirit guides. Find out why spirits haunt us in *True Hauntings*, the only book of its kind written from the perspective of the spirits themselves.

1-56718-218-6, 240 pp., 6 x 9, index, glossary   **$12.95**

JOURNEY OF SOULS
Case Studies of Life Between Lives

Michael Newton, Ph.D.

This remarkable book uncovers—for the first time—the mystery of life in the spirit world after death on earth. Dr. Michael Newton, a hypnotherapist in private practice, has developed his own hypnosis technique to reach his subjects' hidden memories of the hereafter. The narrative is woven as a progressive travel log around the accounts of twenty-nine people who were placed in a state of superconsciousness. While in deep hypnosis, these subjects describe what has happened to them between their former reincarnations on earth. They reveal graphic details about how it feels to die, who meets us right after death, what the spirit world is really like, where we go and what we do as souls, and why we choose to come back in certain bodies.

After reading *Journey of Souls,* you will acquire a better understanding of the immortality of the human soul. Plus, you will meet day-to-day personal challenges with a greater sense of purpose as you begin to understand the reasons behind events in your own life.

1-56718-485-5, 288 pp., 6 x 9　　　　　　　　　　**$14.95**